Jamesian Ambiguity
and *The Sacred Fount*

Jamesian Ambiguity and *The Sacred Fount*

By JEAN FRANTZ BLACKALL

Cornell University Press

Ithaca, New York

For my dear husband Eric, who has stead-
fastly refused to read *The Sacred Fount*

Acknowledgments

I AM especially grateful to Professors Meyer H. Abrams and William M. Sale, Jr., of Cornell and to the reader of this manuscript for the Cornell University Press, who all in various ways have helped me to realize the larger implications of the material.

I am also indebted to the Department of English at Cornell for course relief subsidized by its Grant-in-Aid Fund. And special thanks are due to the librarians of the Olin Library at Cornell for their generous assistance, to Miss Helen Schwartz for her dogged and meticulous checking of hundreds of references and quotations, and to the editors of the Cornell University Press for the care with which they have treated the manuscript.

A substantial part of Chapter 2 is reprinted by permission of the Modern Language Association from *PMLA*, where it appeared in September 1963 under the title *"The Sacred Fount* as a Comedy of the Limited Observer." Professor Leon Edel, Mr. Clifton Waller Barrett, and Miss Anne Freudenberg have made available to me an unpublished James letter; a more specific indication of their assistance appears in Chapter 6. I am consistently indebted to *A Bibliography of Henry James* by Leon Edel and Dan H. Laurence for bibliographical data pertaining to James's works.

JEAN FRANTZ BLACKALL

Ithaca, New York
July 1965

Contents

It is hopeless to try to unravel the threads of the comic and tragic. In James they are the different facets of the same truth. Each light reflects its opposite shadow for those who can see.

ELIZABETH STEVENSON
The Crooked Corridor

MRS. BRISSENDEN: "I mean you're carried away—you're abused by a fine fancy. . . . You build up houses of cards."

The Sacred Fount, p. 262

THE NARRATOR: "Remember . . . that you're costing me a perfect palace of thought!"

The Sacred Fount, p. 311

Jamesian Ambiguity
and *The Sacred Fount*

CHAPTER 1

The Problem in Hand

THERE is no prevailing opinion about what happens in *The Sacred Fount*.[1] Critics have tended, however, to focus on several leading questions: whether the narrator is a detached observer or has a personal stake in the scene he witnesses; whether this anonymous narrator is to be identified with Henry James himself; what the symbolic statement of the novel is; and, finally, whether or not the novel is resolved. The consensus on two of these matters is that the narrator is essentially an observer and that the novel is inconclusive. The narrator is "a week-end guest who seems not to exist in any other capacity whatever except that of week-end guest and who lives vicariously through his fellow guests";[2] or at

---

[1] *The Sacred Fount* (New York: Charles Scribner's Sons, 1901). This text is reproduced in *The Sacred Fount*, intro. Leon Edel (New York: Grove Press, 1953). All subsequent parenthetic page references are to this edition. Initial and terminal ellipses are omitted in quotations from James's text and in other quotations except when such omissions might be confusing.

[2] Edmund Wilson, "The Ambiguity of Henry James," reprinted in *A Casebook on Henry James's "The Turn of the Screw,"* ed. Gerald Willen (New York, 1960), p. 134. Mr. Willen writes of this text: "Edmund Wilson's third (1948) version of 'The Ambiguity of Henry James' is reprinted in full. . . . Mr. Wilson has furnished a postscript, dated 1959, for inclusion in this book" ("Introduction," p. 2).

most he is a " 'prying observer' " [3] or "prying outsider" [4] who "has no personal interest beyond his concern for the integrity of his hypothesis." [5] As for the novel, it is not self-revelatory: "We are asked by Henry James to determine the credibility of the witness, but we are not given enough evidence to arrive at an answer." [6] "While in [Maisie's] case the things she makes out . . . are objectively present for the reader as well, in . . . *The Sacred Fount* the reader has no such assurance." [7] The conclusion, therefore, is "enigmatic," [8] for "the reader is left provided with two complete sets of interpretations of a group of more or less hypothetical relations." [9] "What is prodigious about *The Sacred Fount* is in the mystery that the book encompasses and acknowledges, lucidly and luminously, but which it never reveals, as novels are expected to reveal mysteries, in terms of a plot or a series of actions. It makes its revelation rather in terms of older forms, the forms of the parable, or the fable, or, indeed, of the 'mystery-play.' " [10]

Critics generally agree that *The Sacred Fount* is to be understood as a parable of some sort, but they do not agree about the nature of that parable. Is it "a parable of the use people make of each other"? [11] Or James's "complete and

[3] Edwin T. Bowden, *The Themes of Henry James,* Yale Studies in English, CXXXII (New Haven, 1956), 85.

[4] Adeline R. Tintner, "The Spoils of Henry James," *PMLA,* LXI (March 1946), 247.

[5] Joseph Warren Beach, *The Method of Henry James* (Philadelphia, 1954), p. 88.

[6] Edel, "An Introductory Essay," *The Sacred Fount,* p. xvi.

[7] Frederick W. Dupee, *Henry James,* rev. and enlarged edition, Doubleday Anchor Books (Garden City, N.Y., 1956), p. 168.

[8] Quentin Anderson, *The American Henry James* (New Brunswick, N.J., 1957), p. 121.

[9] Beach, *Method of Henry James,* p. 44.

[10] R. P. Blackmur, "The Sacred Fount," *Kenyon Review,* IV (Autumn 1942), 330–331.

[11] Elizabeth Stevenson, *The Crooked Corridor* (New York, 1949), p. 47.

definitive statement on the subject of love"? [12] Does it drama-
tize the decimating effects of intellectual pride, as a teacher is
consumed by the superior logic he had originally cultivated
in his pupil? [13] Or is it, as the majority have thought until
quite recently, a "parable of life and the artist," [14] "some sort
of fable about the brooding of the imaginative mind and the
material with which it works"? [15] Perhaps "it is . . . one of the
most stupendous parodies ever concocted. . . . It is Henry
James deliberately turning a searchlight on Henry James," [16]
"a self-satire that misfired." [17] Yet, judging from another
point of view, James "took the art of fiction too seriously ever
to burlesque or parody his own practice of it." [18]

To interpret the book as embodying some sort of comment
on the artist or as a self-satire is, of course, to raise the related
questions whether James meant his central figure to stand for
the type of the artist or actually to represent the author himself. Here again opinion has been sharply divided: "True, the
narrator of the novel is not explicitly identified with James
himself. Yet whom else could he conceivably be meant to
represent?" [19] "The 'I' in any [James] story is not Henry
James, not even Henry James disguised." [20] "The hero, the

[12] Osborn Andreas, *Henry James and the Expanding Horizon* (Seattle,
1948), p. 76.

[13] Norma Phillips, *"The Sacred Fount:* The Narrator and the Vampires," *PMLA*, LXXVI (September 1961), 407–412.

[14] Wilson Follett, "Henry James's Portrait of Henry James," *N. Y.
Times Book Rev.* (August 23, 1936), p. 16.

[15] Wilson, "Ambiguity of Henry James," p. 125. In context Mr.
Wilson's statement is speculative.

[16] Follett, "Henry James's Portrait," p. 2.

[17] Dupee, *Henry James*, p. 164.

[18] Edel, "An Introductory Essay," p. vi.

[19] Edward Sackville-West, "Books in General," *New Statesman and
Nation*, XXXIV (October 4, 1947), 273.

[20] Stevenson, *Crooked Corridor*, p. 152.

presiding consciousness, is a novelist. . . . The narrator could be any novelist, and the novelist could in the long run and in the same predicament be any man." [21] Or, rather, might he be the Jamesian prototype of modern man involved in " 'the existential predicament' "? [22]

Faced with such a muddle and diversity of views, one may well ask whether Henry James or his readers are at fault. If critics have failed to arrive even at a tentative agreement on several crucial aspects of the novel, where have they gone astray, who is most to be trusted, and what other perspectives on the novel may bring further insight? If, on the other hand, one concludes, as Edmund Wilson once did, that James himself "was not quite clear about the book in his own mind," [23] is *The Sacred Fount* really worth all the effort? Does the book merely illustrate the fact that James lost his bearings for a while—his sense of the external world and his awareness of the reader's legitimate need for assistance—and therefore produced a work of more potential interest to the biographer than to the student of the novel? These are the questions with which I would like to begin, for I would propose, first, that *The Sacred Fount* is explicable if one submits it to a variety of perspectives out of which cumulative impressions may accrue. On the whole, James has suffered more from his critics than they from him. And yet, it is also true that *The Sacred Fount* gives rise to legitimate perplexities more acute than those deriving from any other James text, and an inquiry into the textual origins of the reader's confusion may therefore direct our attention to some of the origins of Jamesian ambiguity as well. Hence, though the present study is focused

[21] Blackmur, "The Sacred Fount," p. 346.

[22] Robert J. Andreach, "Henry James's *The Sacred Fount:* The Existential Predicament," *Nineteenth-Century Fiction*, XVII (December 1962), 216.

[23] "Ambiguity of Henry James," p. 125.

upon this single most perplexing of all James's texts, I believe that the reader will discover in it both analytic tech-
niques and general implications about James's point of view
and method which are equally pertinent to other texts of the
late period, and especially to those of the nineties.

The first source of difficulty in *The Sacred Fount* is one
with which all readers of *The Awkward Age* are equally familiar. For both books belong to that period in which James
was carrying to an experimental extreme the idea that a novel
might be written like a play, with a minimum of direct
authorial intervention and an extreme reliance upon organic
dialogue to reveal character, relationships, and the very action
itself. Of course such indirectness in narration puts a tremendous demand upon the reader's analytic powers, upon his
memory, and upon his capacity to assimilate conversational
particulars into a mental mosaic of larger scope and significance. And further, the reader must create for his own inner
eye and ear both meaningful postures and character group-
ings, and the intonations with which specific remarks are
delivered, for these are all sources of knowledge to the watcher
of a play.[24]

This whole process is all the more complicated because the
substance of the dialogue within both novels is sustained at
a cerebral and analytic pitch: The characters sustain the same
kinds of mental activities that the reader himself must practice in order to comprehend the novels. Mrs. Brookenham
surrounds herself with a circle of "votaries of analysis," and
these votaries, like the narrator of *The Sacred Fount* in his
dialogues with Mrs. Brissenden, Ford Obert, and others, are
perpetually concerned with getting at the idea of things, with

---

[24] For an extremely interesting illustration of the extent to which
physical attitudes may be apposite to the interpretation of James's fiction, see "The Death of Miles in *The Turn of the Screw*," by Muriel
West, in *PMLA*, LXXIX (June 1964), 283–288.

perceiving the truths that lie behind social façades. However base the matter of their speculations may be, their interest is not merely prurient; they constantly tend, rather, to cerebralize human experience and to render it abstract in order to discover laws and to perceive essences.

Furthermore, in both novels, but especially in *The Sacred Fount,* the reader is forced into the role of arbiter of the views of the characters. Dorothea Krook, in her excellent and lucid analysis of certain origins of ambiguity in *The Sacred Fount,* sees this really as the reader's central problem, that he must come to terms with a substantial number of "independent witnesses" who provide a "rich complication of motives for 'seeing' and 'not seeing.' " Continuing with reference to *The Turn of the Screw,* Mrs. Krook writes: "In *The Sacred Fount* what each principal—including, of course, the narrator—sees and does not see is determined partly indeed by his or her character but chiefly by the relation in which he or she stands, or appears to stand, to the other principals; and since these relations, whether real or delusory, are very much more intricate than those in *The Turn of the Screw,* the motives of the principals are correspondingly more intricate, the incentives to deception and self-deception correspondingly stronger, and the ambiguities springing from these deeper and subtler." [25] *The Sacred Fount,* therefore, with all its assimilative, analytic, and judiciary demands upon the reader, may be understood as a sort of intellectual detective story—but it is important to observe that the reader and not the narrator is the real detective.[26]

---

[25] *"The Sacred Fount," The Ordeal of Consciousness in Henry James* (Cambridge, England, 1962), pp. 173–175 and following.

[26] Oscar Cargill has demonstrated the implausibility of the view that the narrator himself is cast in the role of detective. See *"The Sacred Fount," The Novels of Henry James* (New York, 1961), pp. 288–289.

Insofar as James makes such extreme analytic and assimilative demands upon his reader, *The Sacred Fount* is comparable to *The Awkward Age,* except that, in *The Awkward Age,* for whatever reason—and it may only be that it was conceived and executed as a much longer book—James is more consistently explicit in indicating the attitudes of his characters and the tone in which they speak. He also admits to their company the innocent and uninformed Mr. Longdon, who, coming up to London from the country, is capable of asking explicit and straightforward questions for the reader's edification as well as his own. It would be implausible for the narrator of *The Sacred Fount,* being of the world he contemplates, to be so direct as Mr. Longdon, even if he wished to be. And, in general, the characters peripheral to Mrs. Brookenham are more fully drawn and speak out more explicitly at times than do those who surround the narrator of *The Sacred Fount.* Possibly this effect occurs in part because they speak for themselves and not through the distorting medium of a narrator who interprets and modifies their remarks. *The Awkward Age* seems clearer also because the position of other characters for or against Mrs. Brookenham is more apparent than the relationships of those in *The Sacred Fount* to the narrator, who may not wish to make such attitudes apparent. Nonetheless, to my mind at least, there is nothing in *The Sacred Fount* any more difficult to fathom than there is in many long stretches of *The Awkward Age,* such as Book Sixth, where Mrs. Brookenham's indirection is quintessential.

Hence I would conclude that insofar as James's scenic method is concerned, the book he has written ought not to be beyond the mastery of the discerning reader, provided that he is willing to lavish upon it the kind of patient analysis and constant attention which all late James texts require. If it is at fault, it is so in the same way that most of the experimental novels of the nineties are, that the intellectual acrobatics in which the reader must indulge are out of all proportion to the amount of story and of diversion to be had for the effort. This criticism has of course been leveled at *The Sacred Fount* most brilliantly and caustically by the often quoted Rebecca West, but even sympathetic and discerning readers such as Joseph Warren Beach and Oscar Cargill have afforded the book careful treatment only within the framework of such concepts as "Technical Exercises" and "The Augean Stable." It was something James had to do in order to proceed to something better.[27]

And yet, though technical excesses—in the form of indirect narration and the complexity and abstractness of dialogue— have resulted in *The Awkward Age* being one of James's less popular novels, they have not rendered it virtually inex- plicable, and it has found admirers both for its technical virtuosity and for its marvelous rendering of a transcendent rogue in Mrs. Brookenham herself. Hence we must look further in order to account for the particular hazards which *The Sacred Fount* visits upon the reader, and this brings us to the character of the narrator himself. In *The Awkward Age* we are faced with all sorts of views of the central situation and must weigh and sift the evaluations offered us by char-

[27] General references to the work of other critics refer to the books and articles cited in the Bibliography at the end of this study. In this discus- sion of critics I shall draw most of my examples from studies which have appeared since 1960. For a fuller treatment of earlier criticism see Oscar Cargill's essay in *The Novels of Henry James* and Leon Edel's "Intro- ductory Essay" to the Grove Press reprint of *The Sacred Fount*. There are also notable passages on critical literature pertaining to this novel in Sidney Finkelstein's "The 'Mystery' of Henry James's *The Sacred Fount*," *Massachusetts Review*, III (Summer 1962), 766–772, and in Cynthia Ozick's "The Jamesian Parable: *The Sacred Fount*," *Bucknell Review*, XI (May 1963), *passim*.

acters whose values and degree of self-interest differ. But we are not forced to obtain all our knowledge through the consciousness of any one character, to whose account we are limited and who is both deceitful in the rendering of that account and self-deceiving in his interpretation of the external scene he contemplates. That the narrator is completely unreliable is demonstrable from the text of *The Sacred Fount,* to which I shall turn presently.

But first, why should James have willfully imposed such a character on the reader? Possibly a technical matter was again his chief preoccupation: Was he attempting a sequel to *The Awkward Age* by pushing the scenic method to a still greater experimental extreme? The added hazard for the reader would then be that James not only did not "go behind" his characters, but also interposed between the reader and the action a false witness on whom one might too easily depend. Or can we charge James with sheer perversity and the desire to perplex? He was capable, we know, of teasing his reader's curiosity, for example by refusing to specify the object manufactured in Woollett, Massachusetts. He was capable of indulging in calculated ambiguity in order to enrich the imaginative possibilities of his material, as he does in *The Turn of the Screw* by leaving unspecified the nature of the late servants' wrongdoing. And, in general, most of his stories have something of the appeal and the pitfalls of the detective story for a reason indicated above, that the reader must work things out for himself and find his own way, just as the characters within the novels—Isabel Archer, Strether, Maggie Verver, for example—all must find their way toward larger understandings.

In this instance, however, if James is willfully ambiguous, I suggest that he is so not out of perversity, but because the kind of story he wished to tell required the kind of central

figure he has adopted. This inference is supported partially
by his explanatory letter to Mrs. Humphry Ward, to my
knowledge the one sustained interpretative statement he ever
made about the book. And here let me pause to observe that
Mr. Edel has made the body of this letter available to us in
his second introduction to *The Sacred Fount,* in the Rupert
Hart-Davis reprint of the novel. Since the publication in 1959
of James's statement no critic has discussed any part of it
except the phrases which Mr. Edel quotes in his earlier introduction, to the Grove Press reprint of the novel.[28] From
James's commentary it seems quite clear that he himself saw
the book as fulfilling some compositional law of its own and
that he was perfectly able to explain the relationships and
motives of characters, though he did so, unfortunately, in an
allusive and elliptical way. He also encouraged Mrs. Ward to
look upon the novel as something essentially trivial, as "a
consistent joke," and "the merest of *jeux d'esprit.*" In short,
James's letter does not at all support the idea either that he
was confused about what he was doing or that he desired to
mislead his reader, and it does invite us to look on *The Sacred
Fount* as a joke rather than as something profound.

Let us then turn to the context of the novel, for it is common knowledge that James experimented with point of view
throughout the nineties. And here we immediately discover
two other books, *What Maisie Knew* (1897) and *In the Cage*
(1898), in which the narrative is unfolded from the point of
view of an intrinsically limited observer whose misapprehensions are the stuff of comedy despite intermingling elements
of pathos. The interest of both these stories is largely ironic,
and the irony arises from the discrepancy between the insight or knowledge of an intelligent but not infallible ob-

[28] James's analytic statement is quoted at the beginning of Chapter 6
and followed by my interpretation of it.

server and the things he contemplates. I would suggest that *The Sacred Fount* (1901) represents a third experiment along the same line, a third attempt at a humorous juxtaposing of the views of a limited observer with an objective reality which the reader should be able to perceive for himself. Maisie has limited understanding because she is a child; the telegraphist is similarly restricted by poverty and her social class; and the narrator of *The Sacred Fount,* having both maturity and opportunity to his credit, is handicapped by certain qualities in his character. Perceptive but blinded by pride in his own ingenuity, he is too subtle to interpret accurately the social scene which he witnesses and too proud to admit his perplexities.

If one grants this working hypothesis, that *The Sacred Fount* originated as a kind of experimental sequel to *Maisie* and *In the Cage,* conceived in irony and executed as a comedy of situation, then it may be interpreted, insofar as the plot is concerned, in this way: A man both proud and analytic by disposition undertakes to account for certain characteristics he observes in other persons in terms of a governing concept. Some people are vampires, and others, because they love their respective vampires, are victims. Presently he builds up his concept into an elaborate set of hypotheses to embody all he observes and infers. He becomes so preoccupied with his concept that he throws common sense, sound means of investigation, and good manners to the winds, becoming a snoop, a bore, and the victim of an overriding obsession to perfect and validate his theory. Meanwhile, however, he also begins to feel personal solicitude for the victims and especially for May Server, with whom he falls in love. He would like to declare himself, but his elaborate theory now gets in his way because he believes she is wholly absorbed by her love for one of the vampires and that she could not, therefore, be interested in himself. Hence he must either reject the theory or give up the lady. Because he is a proud man, he chooses to believe that he is right rather than to woo May Server. It is only after he has lost the lady that he begin to realize, under the attacks of another character, that his theory is untrue. But of course this is a compromising situation for a proud man to convey to the reader, and so this narrator records his experience in very oblique terms, trying to seduce the reader into accepting his version of the truth or, at least, into taking him as seriously as he takes himself. James's joke was meant to depend on the reader's gradually being able to see through the narrator, whose willful self-deception would therefore become amusing, and whose downfall would be a satisfying denouement because it is the legitimate reward of a fool. James must have meant initially to tease his reader, to beguile his curiosity, as he does in so many other contexts, but it seems unlikely that he meant to overwhelm the reader with insurmountable ambiguities because the joke depends upon the reader's attaining a dual perspective on the scene he witnesses.

Where James seems to have erred is in underestimating the degree of conviction that this narrator might create in the reader. A child's or a telegraphist's interpretation of the sophisticated world naturally rouses one's critical sense, but the narrator of *The Sacred Fount* is himself a sophisticate. Before he becomes obsessive and progressively absurd, he evinces many of the qualities that Jamesian heroes and heroines also possess. Isabel Archer is no less susceptible to failures of insight in interpreting the behavior and attitudes of others. Mrs. Brookenham and all her crew are equally analytic. And Strether, too, is preoccupied with getting at the truth, even if it should smack of unsavory aspects. But the greatest problem appears to be the degree of cogency that a first-person narrator can summon merely by speaking for himself. Both *In the Cage* and *What Maisie Knew* are third-person narratives, which leaves James somewhat freer to exert an influence even though he gives the reader no more "facts" than are available to the central character. This privilege of modifying the reader's response through interpretative statements, imputations, "asides," and the like, James yields to his character in *The Sacred Fount.*

At this point some of Wayne C. Booth's compelling general conclusions about the positive and ill effects of first-person narration become especially relevant. For, on the one hand, adoption of the first person may reconcile us to a character we would not otherwise tolerate, as Mr. Booth demonstrates in his discussion of another extremely unsympathetic Jamesian hero, John Marcher of *The Beast in the Jungle.* On the other hand, however, the psychological experience of being subjected to "a prolonged intimate view of a character works against our capacity for judgment." [29] The emotional distance between reader and character is narrowed, and the reader tends to yield, submit himself, to the character's point of view. Though I should judge that psychological verisimilitude and the desire to sustain his joke on the narrator through ironic contrasts were James's reasons for electing to write in the first person, he did so, then, at the price of creating sympathy in the reader for a narrator with whom James himself did not sympathize. And *The Sacred Fount* is in this aspect a classic example of the problem which Mr. Booth describes as confusion of distance proceeding from an author's opting for an impersonal form of narration.

The reader's prolonged involuntary subjection to the perspective of a sophisticated, impassioned, and assertive narrator is, then, a second major obstacle in coming to terms with *The Sacred Fount.* There is substantial textual evidence that James consistently set about undercutting the narrator

[29] *The Rhetoric of Fiction* (Chicago, 1961), p. 322.

by indirect means, but indirection seems, in this instance, to have been too subtle a corrective for the conviction that the character could inspire. Nonetheless, practiced readers of James are used to being restricted to the perspectives of central characters who may or may not be reliable; and, for that matter, the most important critical inroads made into *The Sacred Fount* have been directed to pointing up this narrator's limitations. Like the technical exigencies of the book, the duplicity of the narrator is a hazard for the reader, but does not, I believe, sufficiently account for the peculiar difficulties of this text. The ultimate problem, and that which is unique in dealing with any James fiction of this length, is that the development of the *donnée,* which usually occurred in James's *Notebooks,* has in this instance occurred to an uncommon degree during the composition of the book.

The reason that James did not work out his idea in the *Notebooks* seems quite straightforward: it is apparent from his every reference to the "vampire" *donnée* and, later, to the finished book, that he conceived of his material as the stuff of a short story not a novel. Oscar Cargill has observed how unlikely a conception this was, since "here, obviously, are too many elements and possibilities for much compression." [30] But, as every student of James knows, compression in the treatment of the multiple aspects of virtually every idea that touched his imagination was a crucial and central problem for him in all the late fiction. In any event, the short stories frequently require less "working out" in the *Notebooks* than the novels do, and *In the Cage* and *The Sacred Fount* stand alone among later fictions of book length which do not undergo a rather meticulous preliminary development.

In the present instance the story I have so far described is focused upon the character of the narrator, and yet the

[30] *Novels of Henry James,* p. 281.

donnée with which James began deals exclusively with the external scene to which this character is witness. The observer is as yet a nebulous nonentity or a stand-in for the author. If we look at the discussion of *The Spoils of Poynton* in the *Notebooks,* we discover just such a modification of emphasis occurring at a stage prior to composition. In the words of James's editors, "the drama shifts away from their quarrel [that of Owen Gereth and his mother over the property he has inherited] to find its real center in the 'intenser consciousness' of Fleda Vetch," [31] who seemingly stands aloof from their quarrel and yet, whose own prospects are profoundly influenced by it. Wayne Booth again provides us with a larger context in which to view the implications of this kind of switch in emphasis. For he observes how "fascinating [it is] to watch James as he transforms a subject into a story of how it affects or is affected by an observer" [32] and goes on to conclude that "the relationship between his developing narrators and the original subjects was often more complex than his own critical talk recognizes. Some of his stories present, in fact, a double focus that seems to spring from an incomplete fusion of original subject with the new subject that develops once a seriously flawed [i.e., unobjective, biased] narrator has been created to reflect the original." [33] To my sense *The Sacred Fount* is an example of just such an "incomplete fusion" of two subjects. The original subject—the "vampire" *donnée*— gradually becomes for James subsidiary to the mind of the character who conceives it, and yet the prominence accorded the theory in earlier chapters of the book, confirmed by the narrator's protestations of detachment, does not prepare the reader to look elsewhere for an emphasis or a perspective.

[31] *The Notebooks of Henry James,* ed. F. O. Matthiessen and Kenneth B. Murdock (New York, 1947), p. 138.
[32] *Rhetoric of Fiction,* p. 341.   [33] *Ibid.,* p. 346.

If the reader then turns to the *Notebooks* for assistance, his error is compounded. For, unlike the expanded notations for *Poynton,* those for *The Sacred Fount* record a point of departure rather than a concept largely realized, and therefore may encourage the reader to look in the wrong direction; e.g., "[Since] the recent publication of Henry James's notebooks . . . it also becomes clear that the theme of youth feeding age was to have been the real subject of *The Sacred Fount.*" [34] It follows directly from such an assumption about the conclusiveness of the *Notebooks* that the "fine flight . . . *into* the high fantastic" (one of James's descriptive phrases for the book [35]) is actually being enacted in the society of the novel instead of in the narrator's own head, and this is highly misleading. For our response to the concept of the vampirish relationships must be determined largely by our assessment of the character who formulates it, and I stress this point because it seems to me to indicate why *The Sacred Fount* cannot be approached as a simple analogy to other of James's stories in which a vampirish relationship is inherent in the material but in which such a perspective is not imposed.[36] Furthermore, this specific instance of obscurity may be taken as the

[34] Wilson, "Ambiguity of Henry James," p. 145.

[35] Henry James to William Dean Howells, August 9, 1900, *The Letters of Henry James,* ed. Percy Lubbock (New York, 1920), I, 356.

[36] "Osborne's Revenge" (1868) seems to me the nearest real analogy to *The Sacred Fount.* Here Philip Osborne judges Henrietta Congreve, whom he holds responsible for his friend Robert Graham's suicide, in these terms: "There was in her coquetry something serious and exalted. It was an intellectual joy. She drained honest men's hearts to the last drop, and bloomed white upon the monstrous diet." ("Osborne's Revenge," *The Complete Tales of Henry James,* ed. Leon Edel [Philadelphia, 1962], II, 36.) But it is worth noting that the story subsequently reveals that Philip wrongly assessed Henrietta's behavior in relation to his friend.

For another argument against accepting the "vampire" theory at face value, see Oscar Cargill, *Novels of Henry James,* p. 289.

basis for a general caveat to interpreters of James's fiction. Because his critical statements in the *Notebooks* and the prefaces are so consistently helpful in elucidating his fiction, one is sometimes disposed to treat them as dicta or as "whole truths," but James's completed texts often reflect emphases and preoccupations other than those treated in his analytic comments.[37]

The effects of the incomplete fusion, however, are still more complex and diffuse, for not merely "direction" but also tone is affected. The vampire *donnée* as well as the portrait of life or death in Chapter V are inherently the stuff of a serious or somber work, while the character of the narrator and the nature of his adventure, as I have described them, are inherently humorous. James apparently was being torn by contradictory impulses as he proceeded, for he was plagued by the awareness that he was overextending what he considered to be tenuous matter and yet wrote to William Dean Howells that the material exerted upon him a "rank force of its own." [38] He does not explain the nature of this force, and apparently did not wholly understand it himself. My own

[37] Cf. L. C. Knights, writing about *In the Cage* on a matter analogous to the problem in *The Sacred Fount*: "If James is to be blamed for anything it can only be for a misleading phrase in the Preface, where he speaks of the 'solution' depending on the girl's 'winged wit.' 'The action of the drama is simply the girl's "subjective" adventure—that of her quite definitely winged intelligence; just as the catastrophe, just as the solution, depends on her winged wit.' The 'solution' is not, as this might suggest, the solution of Captain Everard's perplexities; it is simply the Telegraphist's recognition—her final acceptance—of the bleakness of reality." ("Henry James and the Trapped Spectator," *Explorations* [New York, 1947], 184.)

Note also the frequency with which the editors of the *Notebooks* point out James's departures from his original notations, and also Mr. Booth's general observation, quoted above, regarding a process of transformation.

[38] December 11, 1902, *Letters*, ed. Lubbock, I, 408.

belief is that in this instance the impulse toward comedy ran away with a potentially serious subject, only to yield in turn to a preoccupation with characterization at a deeper level. Hence in the finished book we have a humorous frame story in which a residue of the *donnée,* a "serious underside," persists as a submerged statement. I shall try to elucidate this process of conversion in my final chapter, after the whole of my interpretation is before the reader. But it is important to observe, meanwhile, the habit of mind out of which these imperfect fusions of subject and observer, sinister and comical aspects, seem to have emerged.

James's capacity and apparent impulse to switch his own point of view to different sides of the same object is the origin both of a three-dimensional effect in his treatment of character (or of situation) and of ambiguities which may obscure his meaning in specific instances. What he gains from switching point of view is not our chief concern here, but we can observe in passing that such characters as Isabel Archer are rounded and lifelike because both their strengths and weaknesses are available to the reader; that a villain like Kate Croy is in part redeemed by her vitality, by her marvelous "talent for life"; and that even the perspectives and motivations of such lesser figures as Henrietta Stackpole or Maria Gostrey are fully represented and the texture of James's books therefore much enriched. Of course James's subtle portraiture even of lesser characters, his avoidance of black-and-white characterization, and the riches that proceed from his willingness to endow his heroines with weaknesses and his villains with redeeming qualities are well known. All goes well so long as we are quite certain who the heroines and villains are, or so long as a character in whom good and bad qualities are subtly intermixed is not in a central position. The Duchess in *The Awkward Age,* for instance, preaches one thing and practices another, but she does not confuse the reader. As a preacher she stands next to Longdon and Vanderbank as a critic of modern London society and in this role is James's spokesman. If she is a hypocrite into the bargain, her duplicity is not especially confusing because the plot does not much depend on whether or not she speaks from self-interest in a given instance. Meanwhile it is amusing for the discriminating reader to perceive, together with Mrs. Brookenham, the Duchess's struggles to play her own little game behind her self-righteous façade.

When we deal with a central figure, however, with a Mrs. Brookenham or a Mme. de Vionnet, the very source of enrichment may become simultaneously a source of perplexing ambiguity, for such figures are corrupt or charming, unforgiveable or a boon to civilized society, depending on which set of criteria the reader adopts—and he is invited to adopt a good many. Likewise the objective situations in which these characters are involved change aspect depending on whether we work from their own points of view or adopt that of another character, a Nanda Brookenham, say, or a Jeanne de Vionnet, whose best interests are antagonistic to those of their mothers. The narrator of *The Sacred Fount* is also such a figure, and his story reflects a divided awareness in James. This narrator is laughable if we see him as a dupe. He is sinister if we contemplate his vampire theory or pause to weigh the serious implications for a human being, and for anyone who becomes personally involved with him, of his self-deceiving approach to life. Hence the book is inconsistent in tone as well as in the general direction of its development, and these inconsistencies are a third, and perhaps the most taxing, source of difficulty for the reader. Because James constantly perceived multiple facets of the same characters and situations, and because he realized so fully the points of view even

of lesser and of unsympathetic characters, he faces his reader
at all times with a demanding task of discriminating emphases. This problem is compounded in the fiction of the
experimental period because in these books "roundedness"
of representation occurs in conjunction with experiments in
point of view and scenic method. For the sake of psychological verisimilitude and of dramatic effect James has withdrawn, or rendered very indirectly, much of the authorial
support that he provides in his earlier fiction and again in
the latest books. In *The Sacred Fount* the problem is still
more acute because James seems not wholly to have perceived
the degree to which contradictory impulses in himself during
composition might distort or obscure his emphasis.

James's presumptive lack of awareness of this source of
difficulty for the reader is a consequence, I believe, of the fact
that the book does reveal an emphasis, on the humorous,
which surprisingly critics *en masse* have not perceived. And
of those few who have perceived this aspect of the book,
only Wilson Follett has elected to incorporate it into an over-
all concept of what the book is about. Why should this be so?
First, perhaps, because James has made so heavy an intellectual demand on his reader, one supposes that one is to be
richly rewarded for the effort. There *must* be depths to be
fathomed! Then, the narrator is himself a very convincing
figure; in part, as I have speculated, for reasons which suited
James's purpose and in part, apparently, because James was
unintentionally ambiguous in surrendering his reader to this
dominating intelligence. Furthermore, the most salient, if not
the most pervasive, aspects of the book, the theory and the
portrait, are also the most sinister, and James's statements in
the *Notebooks* encourage us to regard them as central. Hence
critics seem generally to have begun with an assumption that
the book must be profound—and this is the first general
assumption which I would call into question. All the numer-

ous misguided attempts to treat the narrator as a type of the artist or the novelist or, still worse, to equate him with Henry James, naturally follow from this assumption of profundity. A second misleading assumption is that, whatever *The Sacred Fount* may be, labyrinth or parable, it is all one thing and that therefore one can account for its meaning or total effect by some governing concept that will explain the whole. Since no one concept, no statement of a serious parable certainly, embraces both the comical and the serious aspects of the novel, critics have therefore had to move at varying degrees above the text or to deal only with those portions of it which most satisfactorily sustain their respective views—and this tendency has led to a general neglect of some of the most rudimentary structural and verbal aspects of the novel.

We are all in the fog together, and I do not wish to abuse individual studies unduly. But this kind of detached perspective on *The Sacred Fount* is clearly illustrated in an article by Parker Tyler, who is not sufficiently mindful either of the text or of any pre-existing critical statement. Mr. Tyler, contemplating the narrator's "sense of identification" with Mrs. Server, speculates that *"The Sacred Fount* might well be a parable of Henry James's own erotic experience: a mighty speculation-in-little about the terms on which he has escaped giving himself in love, which might be the same as those on which he has been able to retain his belief in the unlimited powers of love *as intelligence*." [39] He concludes, in any case, that "simply by equating a Rhoda Broughton with a Mrs. Humphry Ward, he would logically have arrived at a Mrs. Briss." [40] And the narrator's final dialectical bout with Mrs. Briss over the validity of his theory may therefore be taken

[39] *"The Sacred Fount:* 'The Actuality Pretentious and Vain' vs. 'The Case Rich and Edifying,' " *Modern Fiction Studies,* IX (Summer 1963), 136.
[40] *Ibid.,* p. 135.

as an ironic representation of James's drawing-room experience of sustaining intellectual attacks from less subtle and
sensitive persons:

> I find the scene, therefore, full of an exquisitely affecting and
> expressive pathos, and all the more so because it is an anti-climax
> for the growth of that fond intimacy between himself and Mrs.
> Briss which I have called a "flirtation." Indeed, it may be the very
> model of James's actual "literary flirtations" with his distinguished
> women readers. How romantic and how extravagant, then, is Mrs.
> Briss's savage "intelligence." Each new blow becomes harder; one
> feels them in poor HJ's midriff. The Mrs. Briss of fiction, if not
> the Mrs. Briss of life, is trying for a knockout. Technically, too,
> she may achieve one. But the Narrator, as James's *persona,* does
> not take it, I think, lying down.[41]

Whatever the dominant tone of the concluding scene may
be, it is certainly not covered by the concept of pathos. And
one can only wonder why, if Mrs. Ward had recently been
pummeling him in the midriff, James subsequently felt the
impulse to write her the playful and sustained elucidation of
the novel which Mr. Edel has made available to us. But the
root issue here—and one which is equally pertinent in assessing Mr. Follett's idea that the novel is a self-parody of the
artist, and Maxwell Geismar's treatment of the novel as a
psychological gold mine in which to delve for James's sexual
attitudes—is simply that of whether or not the identification
of James with specific characters is ever a fruitful critical approach. And I can only second the view of Mr. Cargill, who,
speaking from a very wide knowledge of relevant secondary
literature, concludes that "those scholars and critics who have
read James primarily for a revelation of the secret self . . .
have been the most tasteless. James offered his work, not himself, for consumption, and they have not been about the main
business. Too many clairvoyants practise criticism." [42] James

[41] *Ibid.,* p. 133.   [42] *Novels of Henry James,* p. xii.

is not nearly so simple-minded as this kind of identification makes him seem, and he is neither Longdon nor Strether nor the narrator of *The Sacred Fount*.[43]

But to return to the question of emphasis: In all the secondary literature on *The Sacred Fount*, I have come upon only a handful of critics who have even flirted with the idea that it is amusing. F. W. Dupee elliptically seconds Wilson Follett's concept: "evidently a self-satire that misfired." [44] Maxwell Geismar also seconds Mr. Follett, attributing "humor" to James which finds expression in "satire and self-satire," [45] but his subsequent reading of the novel does not convey the idea that it is even remotely amusing. Sidney Finkelstein perceives a "light and witty tone" [46] in the earlier part of the novel, but sees this as yielding to something more somber as the story progresses. He is right, I believe, so far as he goes, but since our divergences center in the interpretation of the figurative language of the novel, I will return to his excellent article in Chapter 3. Wayne Booth goes somewhat further. Discussing "confusion about moral and spiritual problems," he writes: "Why should James not be able to write as great a book on the theme of *The Sacred Fount* as on that of *The Ambassadors?* The quest of a male gossip for a clear picture of the amatory pairings of a group of weekend guests is simply not as important as the quest of Strether for the meaning of life itself. Even if, by some miracle of will, James had been able to bring himself to develop *The Sacred*

[43] Cf. the conclusion of Ralph A. Ranald in *"The Sacred Fount:* James's Portrait of the Artist *Manqué,"* *Nineteenth-Century Fiction,* XV (December 1960), 242–243.

For the most recent, amplified and involuted, version of the basic theory of parody, see Laurence Bedwell Holland's interpretation in *The Expense of Vision* (Princeton, 1964).

[44] *Henry James,* p. 164.

[45] *Henry James and the Jacobites* (Boston, 1963), p. 199.

[46] "The 'Mystery' of Henry James's *The Sacred Fount,"* p. 759.

Fount with anything like the fulness of *The Ambassadors,* it would take another miracle of *our* wills to make us care about the first quest as much as the second." [47]

In passing, one might question this characterization of the novel, for the narrator is no simple gossip. One reason for his confusion (and ours) is that he confides too little in others to adjust and correct his own views of things. Secondly, this is a description of one possible effect the narrator creates on a detached observer rather than a characterization of the stated nature of the narrator's interest and quest. His interest, as I have observed above, is neither sensational nor prurient; it is the idea of things—in his own words, "the vision of life" (23)—that he strives to attain. Because he strives unwisely he is a comical figure, a kind of parodistic counterpart to Strether, whose humility and receptiveness to the views of others in large part exempt him from those pitfalls to which this narrator is liable. Or better yet, he is a comical counterpart to John Marcher, in whose story, as Mr. Booth observes, the tragic implications of egoism are touched upon.[48]

Nonetheless "amatory pairings" *are* a peculiar vehicle for metaphysical researches, and Mr. Booth goes on to point out where a book dependent on such matter is likely to lead us: "It should go without saying that a great comedy could be written about the quest of a male gossip for a clear picture of the amatory pairings of a group of weekend guests. James at times approaches this kind of comedy in *The Sacred Fount,* but he approaches it only to shift back into something else, something that seems to be trying for profundity and that in the trying ruins itself." [49] What the "something else" that adulterates comical effect in *The Sacred Fount* may be, I will return to later, but first let us establish that such an effect

---

[47] *Rhetoric of Fiction,* pp. 292–293.   [48] *Ibid.,* p. 279.
[49] *Ibid.,* p. 293 n.

may exist. D. W. Jefferson, who does not pretend to offer an inclusive interpretation of the novel, yet is a reader most sensitive to its humorous aspects, e.g., "Transcendental verbiage mingles with the open zest of the scandalmonger." [50] Miss Cynthia Ozick has approached the same matter rather obliquely. For in justly arguing, in company with Leon Edel, Edmund Wilson, and others, against the theory that the book is a self-parody, she observes that James would never indulge in so blatant a form of humor as "an open-faced hoax, with its joke in its mouth." She offers us an excellent description of some of the subtler guises in which Jamesian humor reveals itself: "James's comic eye, the *matériel* of his deeper humor, so often overlooked, his cannonades of wit, his buried verbal gags, the indefatigable undertow of his subtleties and ironies and satiric currents, are not the kind of 'fun' (a word he uses often and enjoys) that characterizes the puller of hoaxes." [51] But here, alas, Miss Ozick turns from the application of this statement to *The Sacred Fount* with only a parenthetic remark, "a not absolutely humorless book, by the way," [52] and then proceeds, in the company of so many other earnest critics, to argue that the book is profound and a parable. Beyond these writers, no one seems to have been amused, even tentatively, except that Mrs. Krook has accounted for the irony that she perceives in the novel as James's means of achieving a light touch in dealing with profound matter:

My own view, like Mr. Edel's, is that it is James's most serious and most exhaustive study of the creative imagination, and of the moral and philosophical difficulties inherent in its characteristic operations. It is not a parody but an analysis, an elucidation, an anatomy; and what is most likely to have misled Mr. Follett into

[50] *Henry James and the Modern Reader* (New York, 1964), p. 179.
[51] "The Jamesian Parable," p. 57.   [52] *Ibid.*, pp. 57–58.

seeing it as he does is the deceptive lightness of touch with which the anatomy is conducted. The Jamesian irony, unfalteringly urbane, ensures the consistent absence of solemnity; and it is rendered the more deceptive by the Jamesian energy in the pursuit of the analytic task itself, and the sustained fascination ('amusement') at all that the process of analysis yields to the enquiring mind.[53]

But of course all these various attempts to allow for wit, incongruity, and ludicrous excess in the novel simply intimate where James's emphasis lies. This narrator is not Prince Hamlet nor was meant to be—and that is why he can erect so subtle an intellectual structure, rife with metaphysical and moral implications, upon an inquiry which is sustained in activities so pedestrian as to be socially reprehensible. The immense discrepancy between the explicit nature of the narrator's activities—snooping and gossiping—and the rarified intellectual preoccupations to which he aspires ought at least to give the reader pause. Why should a character who has seemed a snoop and a bore to so many readers, one whose excesses might even give rise to the idea of parody, be adopted by James to support a thoughtful artistic, moral, or metaphysical statement when James was capable of creating a Longdon and a Strether in the two novels he wrote immediately before and after this one? This would be a remarkable illustration of urbanity.

Furthermore, the whole texture of *The Sacred Fount is* permeated with equally ludicrous incongruities. There is the distance between the narrator's complex theory and a common-sense view of the things he scrutinizes. Why accept anything so preposterous when *passim* all the other characters at least intimate more straightforward explanations both through their behavior and their remarks? There is the ridic-

[53] Krook, *Ordeal of Consciousness*, p. 183.

ulous turkey metaphor in which the narrator elaborates the
first and principal statement of his theory:

"Mrs. Briss [one of the vampires] had to get her new blood,
her extra allowance of time and bloom, somewhere; and from
whom could she so conveniently extract them as from Guy [her
husband] himself? She *has,* by an extraordinary feat of legerde-
main, extracted them; and he, on his side, to supply her, has had
to tap the sacred fount. But the sacred fount is like the greedy
man's description of the turkey as an 'awkward' dinner dish. It
may be sometimes too much for a single share, but it's not enough
to go round."

Obert was at all events sufficiently struck with my view to
throw out a question on it. "So that, paying to his last drop, Mr.
Briss, as you call him, can only die of the business?"   (29–30)

If this narrator is seriously contemplating a relationship involving life and death, how can he do so in terms so inadequate without our ascribing to James—who was ever mindful
of the right word—either an egregious lapse in diction or a
bad joke? If we then turn to the metaphorical language of the
novel generally, we find that the narrator's gravity is constantly undercut by compromising metaphors, all the more
deliciously ironic because James has made the first-person
narrator inadvertently testify against himself. Finally, James
seems almost to drop his own mask when he inserts into one
of the narrator's self-congratulatory interior monologues a
compromising topical allusion (never so identified by critics)
of no substantive relevance to its context. This allusion appears to be there solely to influence the reader's attitude toward the interpretation of the passage, and it encourages the
idea that the narrator is a superlative crackpot.

A thoroughgoing demonstration of the presence of these
four kinds of incongruity which permeate the fabric of *The
Sacred Fount* will constitute my next three chapters. Chapter

2 treats the incongruity between the narrator's self-image and a more objective view, and that between his fantastical theory and other interpretations more firmly anchored in common sense, plausibility, or logic. Chapter 3 considers the discrepancy between the narrator's own accounts of his progress and the more revealing figurative undercurrents, and Chapter 4 attempts to recreate the effect which James must have supposed the topical allusion would have for his contemporary readers. I shall be at some pains to elucidate all these possible perspectives that bring us, ultimately, to similar conclusions, because it seems to me that James's own perspective in the novel is revealed through cumulative effect, through a pervasiveness of ironic incongruity. It is these verbal aspects of the novel, and especially the function of figurative and allusive language, which have been too frequently ignored by critics or which have been subjected to partial or fragmented examination. And it is from this collective weight of textual evidence that I derive the plot outlined above, which I am sure the reader will agree is inherently amusing—just as amusing, say, as the tribulations of Arnolphe in Molière's *Éçole des Femmes*.

Still, as I have already observed, a very substantial work has been performed in exposing the narrator, especially since Oscar Cargill's illuminating chapter on *The Sacred Fount* appeared in 1960. Basing his argument on an earlier and neglected speculation by Philip Littell, Mr. Cargill asks: "In *The Spoils of Poynton,* in *What Maisie Knew,* and in *The Awkward Age* (to say nothing about shorter things) James tried out various points of view; why not suppose that he continued his trials with *The Sacred Fount* and regard it as his experiment with telling a story through a narrator who has an obsession?" [54] Why not, indeed? Since Mr. Cargill's

[54] *Novels of Henry James,* p. 283.

book appeared, a number of articles have been published which tend collectively to develop the view expressed by him, and earlier by Mr. Edel in his first introduction to the novel, that the narrator is not wholly admirable as a character: He is obsessive, yes, and he is turned in upon himself. Sometimes he is irrational, sometimes imperceptive, sometimes makes false surmises. He is proud. Notable among the cases against the narrator are those by Miss Norma Phillips and Robert Andreach, who expose him on both logical and personal grounds.

But surprisingly this increased awareness of the limitations of the character has not dissipated the idea that *The Sacred Fount* embodies a serious statement, even a parable. If *The Sacred Fount* is not a "straight" parable about how the artist works, yet may it be an epistemological statement? Granted that this narrator is limited and susceptible to failures of insight, may his very perplexity and desperate excess illustrate the struggles of the inquiring mind to distinguish appearance and reality? (Mrs. Krook and, earlier, Mr. Edel.) May he, therefore, in a larger sense, be modern man involved in an existential dilemma? "It is impossible that James did not know that he was creating a narrator whose logical apprehension of the world interferes with his real experiencing of it. The narrator's language and thought processes are too complex, his isolation too acute, to be the work of an artist unconscious of the predicament of modern man, . . . 'the existential predicament.' " [55] Or, alternatively, we are asked to conclude that *The Sacred Fount* is "a study in logic and semiosis," [56] in which understanding is not the principal con-

---

[55] Andreach, "Henry James's *The Sacred Fount*," p. 216.
[56] Joseph Wiesenfarth, "*The Sacred Fount* and the Perspective of Achievement," *Henry James and the Dramatic Analogy: A Study of the Major Novels of the Middle Period* (New York, 1963), p. 97.

sideration. In Brother Wiesenfarth's view, reminiscent of that of Joseph Warren Beach, "The *Fount* is not concerned with truth, but with the correct reasoning about signs. . . . [It] is, basically, a novel which represents the process of imaginative fabrication of a 'structure' from a 'germ' that has been conceived as a 'subject.' The fascination of *The Sacred Fount* lies in the building of the structure; the climax of the novel comes when Grace Brissenden faces the narrator with another structure which opposes his. And the book ends with the reader's looking at two structures, neither of which he can choose with certainty, but both of which he has reason to regard as probable." [57] If we then combine the idea that *The Sacred Fount* is concerned with the fabrication of logical structures with the idea that it may illustrate the functioning of the artist, we arrive at the subtler and very cogent rendering of a similar position recently offered by Tony Tanner:

The narrator certainly epitomizes the artistic instinct for James. The initial line of his inquiry—is Gilbert Long having an affair which is in some way nourishing him with unexpected energy at the expense of some unknown suffering woman?—extends to the whole question of discerning or imposing a principle of order in or on the world. He talks about his theory very much as many critics have talked about a work of art; 'that special beauty of my scheme through which the whole depended so on each part and each part guaranteed the whole.' He wants and works to elicit a golden world from the brazen world—not however a world where people are better than in our world but a world in which their lives have more logic and shape. . . .

If 'art is our flounderings shown' as Colonel Voyt suggests in *The Story in it,* then the narrator's attempt to chart the tangled relations of the people around him has at least the value of drawing up a tentative map for a troubled sea. Even if the flounderings

[57] *Ibid.,* pp. 97, 102.

are due to the ineradicable predatory instincts of men and women
—still it is better to have a pattern of pursuit and carnage than no
pattern at all. . . .

It is perhaps the aim of all artists to 'separate things from chaos'
and we could say that the intention of the narrator of *The Sacred
Fount* is to take his raw material from the social world and reform
it into a more orderly dispensation.[58]

As I see it, the fault with such speculations—with the idea
that the novel either renders the artist's or "man's" attempts
to discern reality or to order experience—is that they depend
on our making either or both of two inhibiting assumptions:
that we can be no wiser than the narrator and that the book
is unresolved, except, perhaps, as a kind of logically ingenious
construct devoid of a conclusion other than that which form
imposes. We must share in the narrator's perplexity in order
to see in him a prototype either of the artist or of ourselves
perplexed. And we must be prepared to accept the idea that
James would go so far in divorcing abstract form from ultimate meaning. Is there a single other instance in which he has
let logic pass for substance? And when James himself (as
distinguished from his narrator here) is in the role of artist,
his created worlds consistently intimate operative moral criteria as well as offering a "map" or an "orderly dispensation
of the raw materials of life." His villains, like their victims,
suffer for their misdoing (e.g., Mme. Merle, Mrs. Brookenham, Kate Croy, Charlotte Stant), and I can think of no
other novel of James's in which a pattern of carnage is offered
us devoid of practical as well as symbolic consequences. Even
Rose Armiger, who suffers no legal consequences, is deprived
of the objective for which she was capable of committing

[58] "Henry James's Subjective Adventurer: 'The Sacred Fount,'" *Essays
and Studies,* XVI (London, 1963), 44, 48, 54.

murder, and in general James's villains experience either frustration or remorse. According to this argument the villains go scot free; they are merely the objects of an impotent scrutiny on the part of a disapproving "artist" narrator. J. A. Ward observes the consistency with which James ironically employs the theme of salvation in the fiction of the middle period, so that a character who is apparently good or who intends good may become the instrument of evil, for example the telegraphist of *In the Cage* or the governess of *The Turn of the Screw,* and he places the narrator of *The Sacred Fount* in this company. But this is not tantamount to saying that James would create a hero who exerts no practical effect except a sympathetic attitude. I cannot go along with Mr. Ward's subsequent equation of the narrator's "knowledge" with action.[59]

If, on the other hand, we take up the idea of Mr. Blackmur —which has recently been tacitly accepted by Tony Tanner and very ably developed by Mr. Finkelstein—that the narrator functions as a conscience, creating a painful awareness in both the supposed vampires, we must at least observe that he also creates discomfiture in every one else at the house party because of his tactics.[60] Hence he becomes indiscriminately an agent of punishment to Mrs. Server whom he champions and to Mrs. Brissenden whom he judges. The narrator does not merely "introduce into the callous indifference of unconscious life a sense of good things spoiled and cruelties perpetrated"; [61] he himself spoils good things, as I shall be at pains to demonstrate. And here again, I think that we have no other instance in James's fiction of a reformative

[59] See J. A. Ward, "The Ineffectual Heroes of James's Middle Period," *Texas Studies in Literature and Language,* II (Autumn 1960), *passim.*
[60] Cf. pp. 48–49 and 81–83, below.
[61] Tanner, "Henry James's Subjective Adventurer," p. 49.

agent's discomfiting the innocent—e.g., Mrs. Wix in her relationship to Maisie, and the governess in her relationship to
Flora and Miles—except as a consequence of limited understanding, obsession, or the incapacity to cope. Whether we
see the narrator as totally aloof or as a "conscience," we have
a book in which normal cause and effect in moral terms is
functioning peculiarly. This *could* of course indicate a new
degree of astringency in James's outlook on the corruptions
of modern society. But since James has given us a great many
inducements to see through and beyond the narrator, the
more plausible assumption is that we should adopt criteria
other than those the narrator offers us, e.g., common sense
and a sense of the ridiculous. When we do so it becomes
possible to discern a good many objective realities of his
world without recourse to his theory, as Sidney Finkelstein
and Oscar Cargill, more than anyone else to date, have done
in their admirable essays. One can perceive, for instance, that
the narrator is not merely an observer in the novel but a participant within the story; that he suffers the consequences of
his own misconceptions; that, however high his declared motives, his misconceptions also cause pain to the innocent (in
keeping with Mr. Ward's observation that in these middle
period books good purposes may be aborted to evil ends);
and that through the narrator, in keeping with more usual
Jamesian patterns of moral cause and effect, the vampires are
punished through fear. But all of this will become clearer in
subsequent chapters.[62]

Meanwhile, as the penultimate sentence implies, I do not

[62] For some other objections to the "conscience" thesis as it was
originally expressed by Mr. Blackmur, see Oscar Cargill, *Novels of
Henry James,* pp. 285–286, and Cynthia Ozick, "The Jamesian Parable,"
pp. 64–66. For a more particular criticism of the theory that the novel
specifically embodies a statement about the artist's experience, see pp.
112–117, below.

mean to say that there are not serious implications to be drawn from *The Sacred Fount* for the reasons enumerated above: self-delusion is amusing so long as we do not contemplate its effects upon the individual and those involved with him, but when we do, our amusement is short-lived. We may genuinely see in this narrator both an exemplar and a victim of the sin of intellectual pride (Miss Phillips' view, and that of James K. Folsom). We may see in his society inherent decay (Mr. Finkelstein and Mr. Cargill). But these things are not James's *emphasis.* If they were, *The Sacred Fount* would have become *The Awkward Age* with John Marcher for a hero. In *The Awkward Age* the indictment of society is explicit and sustained, and in both stories the sufferings of the victims, Nanda and May Bartram, are contemplated at close range and in some detail. Their points of view are more fully and more consistently elucidated. *The Sacred Fount* is perhaps moving in that direction, as I have tried to allow for in speaking of its "serious underside." But it was never conceived as a formulated parable, any more than *What Maisie Knew* or *In the Cage* was, and readers have been looking at the underside of the carpet!

Nonetheless, having expressed this reservation about emphasis—one which I trust the substance and proportions of my essay will more conclusively demonstrate—I now join the happy throng. For, concluding that the book was conceived and executed as high comedy, I find myself in agreement with the great majority of critics who have found in *The Sacred Fount* some kind of unplumbed depths, and my own version of this deeper meaning is proposed in Chapter 5. But such meaning seems to me to constitute a submerged statement, adumbrated rather than realized, symbolic and highly figurative in its expression, and perhaps not wholly evolved by James himself until the writing of *The Ambassadors* in the following year. For *The Sacred Fount* has interesting thematic affinities with both *The Portrait of a Lady* and *The Ambassadors,* as well as with some of the shorter pieces.

By now the reader will have discerned the criteria, or the multiple perspectives, rather, according to which I conclude that *The Sacred Fount* will yield to analysis, and those according to which I believe that individual interpretations of the novel can be assessed: Which interpretation is most inclusive? Which incorporates most of the fabric of the novel, dealing with all of the cruxes such as the mysterious portrait, the concept of the sacred fount, the question of tone, that of the obsessive aspects of the narrator's character, the question of the book's resolution, and so forth? Which moves closest to the text? Which can be harmoniously explained with specific reference to James's own comments about the novel, both those in the *Notebooks* and those in his personal correspondence? For we have no grounds for believing that he wished to mislead either William Dean Howells, the Duchess of Sutherland, or, especially, Mrs. Humphry Ward, who appears to have written him a serious letter of inquiry. What "proofs" can I myself offer? In turn, I have constructed my essay with reference to these same criteria, and I should suppose that inclusiveness and cumulative effect would be my best arguments.

For these reasons I have allowed this study to run to such length, believing that *The Sacred Fount,* like all of James's late fiction, can reveal itself only through the invocation of multiple perspectives, and believing, too, that any attempt to place it in the James canon requires our seeing it in some sort of total perspective. For, aside from producing what I hope will prove to be a cogent and inclusive explication of this most problematic of all James's novels, I believe that my prolonged sojourn in the jungle has suggested a more important perspective in which to examine the novel than that merely of a brain-teaser or an experimental failure. No one would argue that any book which has so consistently failed to reveal itself even to the most patient and practised of readers is wholly successful, and it is clear from his correspondence that James himself was dissatisfied with it. If we desire an example of restricted point of view or of scenic technique, there are more effective experiments elsewhere. But it is the last book of James's experimental period, and possibly for that reason it reflects, more than any other work of the nineties, the complex and kaleidoscopic transitional state of mind out of which the great later novels were to emerge. My sixth chapter was originally conceived to illustrate how anyone might conclude that the same book could be both high comedy and profound statement, but perhaps it will also afford, together with this present statement of the nature of the problems which confront the reader, a speculative insight into some of the mental processes out of which *The Sacred Fount* must have grown. And perhaps *The Sacred Fount* may best take its place in the James canon beside the more calculated and analytic statements in the *Notebooks* and the Prefaces as a source of insight into the mental processes of the artist. For it appears to illustrate an intuitive and partially conscious effort, not to perceive reality, and not merely to create a structure of words, but the effort to shape reality into an artistic form which would both mirror life and inform it with meaning.

CHAPTER 2

The Social Adventure
of the Narrator

THE SACRED FOUNT is an intellectual detective story, as has often been observed, and much of its interest consists in the investigation of a hypothetical problem. If it is true, as the narrator speculates, that a vampirish relationship exists between one couple, may an analogous relationship exist between another couple, and who is the second member of that second pair? But to discover the answer to this question the reader must assume a relationship to the book comparable to the narrator's relationship to other characters within it, and observe for himself. For the objective measures of the credibility of the witness that are generally lacking within the novel, he must substitute his own insights. Certain of the sources of insight available to him are: the remarks and manifest attitudes (both mental and physical) of other characters, the reader's own opinion of how the narrator's behavior might be expected to affect other persons, his estimate of the logic of the narrator's thought processes, the figurative language of the book, and the revealing topical allusion—all matters which we shall consider in this and the two following chapters.

The book is technically so complex, and its meaning so

consistently problematical, that I propose first to trace the plot, or social adventure of the narrator, without reference to its symbolic implications. But this process is by no means so straightforward as the plot outline offered on pages 11–12 above would suggest. From the opening pages of *The Sacred Fount* the reader is striving—more or less consciously depending on how easy he finds it to accept the narrator's account of things—to distinguish an objective "truth" from the views of that truth presented by the narrator and by his various interlocutors. Hence the story moves vertically, so to speak, as well as horizontally. Reading the novel is largely an analytic process, and understanding it, a retrospective one. The reader is constantly reassessing or discovering new facets of earlier scenes, and he must sometimes pause to consider what is assumed but left unsaid between the characters. In this chapter I shall attempt to communicate something of this effect of reading the book, presenting insights in an order in which they might naturally occur to the reader while simultaneously demonstrating the analytic and assimilative processes requisite to arrive at a conclusion. One may object that this whole method of reading is too formalized and analytic, that James could not have demanded any such participation from his reader. But the excessive intellectualizing in *The Sacred Fount* arises from the character James has created: "He is addicted . . . to the intellectualizing of every human situation; he seems to be prey to anxieties unless he can achieve a kind of intellectual superiority and omniscience over those around him. It is this which makes him feel secure." [1] And this kind of excess, though perhaps more palatable to James himself as a form of intellectual diversion than it is to many of his readers, is nonetheless one of the means by which the narrator betrays himself. To catch the narrator, therefore, as well as

[1] Leon Edel, *The Psychological Novel 1900–1950* (New York, 1955), p. 71.

to arrive at an objective estimate of what happens in the story, the reader must doggedly meet him on his own ground.

The first two chapters constitute a prologue to the central portion of the book. They are separated from the following chapters in time, recording the events that occur on the first day of a week-end house party at Newmarch, from early afternoon until bedtime. The rest of the novel will treat continuously the events of the second day, extending into the early hours of the third. In these two chapters all the principal characters are introduced. The narrator is shown in the process of passing from incredulousness and mild indifference into a state of intense interest in the first of the couples he will consider. The elements in his character that will be significant in judging his subsequent insights are suggested. And, most important, at the end of Chapter II he meticulously spells out to a friend the theory that he has formed as a basis for subsequent inquiry.

During this first afternoon and evening the narrator is subject to four unexpected impressions. At Paddington Station he notices a former week-end acquaintance, Gilbert Long, but does not expect Long to speak to him: "I had met him at Newmarch only . . . but he had always, in the interval, so failed to know me that I could only hold him as stupid unless I held him as impertinent. He was stupid in fact" (2). On this occasion, however, Long approaches the narrator and makes himself so agreeable that the narrator is forced to revise his opinion: "His manners had distinctly gained in ease" (3). In their subsequent conversation Long continues to seem cleverer than he has ever appeared before (7). A second surprise occurs at Paddington. The narrator fails to recognize Grace Brissenden, a former acquaintance, until she speaks: "I reflected that she might easily have thought me the same sort of ass as I had thought Long" (3).

Most of the first chapter is composed of two conservations

which the narrator has an opportunity to hold with each of his companions separately before the three ride down together to Newmarch. In the first Gilbert Long eagerly confirms the narrator's reaction to Grace Brissenden: " 'I didn't place her at first myself. She had to speak to me. . . . She's amazing for her age' " (5). They conclude that, forty-two or -three, Mrs. Brissenden looks younger than her husband, who " 'isn't yet thirty' " (5). Long volunteers the two principal insights to be drawn from their mistake, first, that Mrs. Brissenden isn't handsomer or finer, but younger in proportion to her years: " 'Her clock has simply stopped. She looks no older—that's all' " (6). The narrator, weighing the matter, accepts Long's point: " 'I take your discrimination . . . as just' " (6). Long then points the moral, exaggerating slightly for emphasis: " 'It wouldn't have mattered to [Guy Brissenden] if she had [flaunted her fifty years]. That's the awfulness, don't you see? of the married state. People have to get used to each other's charms as well as to their faults. He wouldn't have noticed. It's only you and I who do, and the charm of it is for *us*' " (7).

The second conversation, with Mrs. Brissenden, parallels the first in that she concurs with the narrator's revised estimate of Long. "She put it to me frankly that she had never seen a man so improved: a confidence that I met with alacrity, as it showed me that, under the same impression, I had not been astray" (8). Mrs. Brissenden proposes a reason for the change. A clever woman, perhaps Lady John, has Long in hand. She even suggests that Lady John's coming down today on a different train with Guy Brissenden is a little subterfuge, the appearance of a friendship cultivated to cover another friendship. She concludes: " 'If she hasn't made him clever, what has she made him? She has given him, steadily, more and more intellect' " (10). " 'Well, you may be right,' " the narrator laughs, " 'though you speak as if it were cod-liver

oil. Does she administer it, as a daily dose, by the spoonful?' "
(10–11). And he remains skeptical: " 'The difficulty for me is
simply that if I've seen the handsome grow ugly and the ugly
handsome, the fat grow thin and the thin fat, the short grow
long and the long short; if I've even, likewise, seen the clever,
as I've too fondly, at least, supposed them, grow stupid: so
have I *not* seen—no, not once in all my days—the stupid grow
clever' " (11).

At Newmarch later that afternoon the narrator is mildly
curious but not impatient at first. He refers to the narrative
he is unfolding as an "anecdote" (5, 13) and a "riddle" (15),
prompting the reader to regard the story as a diversion rather
than a serious matter. Now he will proceed to record "the
happiest little chapter of accidents" (13). Two of these accidents at Newmarch happen to resemble those which occurred
earlier at Paddington: May Server is, in the eye of the painter
Ford Obert, changed; but the narrator cannot see why Obert
should think so and is critical of the reasons he proposes. Why
should Obert feel that May Server is unhappy? Or be frightened that she was perhaps making love to him? Wasn't he
aware, Obert persists, that she later made love to the narrator too? "I didn't know that I had been. 'Not to the point
of terror. She's so gentle and so appealing' " (19). The narrator is detached, beguiled perhaps but frankly skeptical.
His attitude is comparable to that he held toward Mrs. Brissenden's proposal that Gilbert Long drew wit from Lady
John.

What rouses him much more is his subsequent failure to
recognize Guy Brissenden: "I . . . reflected on the oddity of
my having been as stupid about the husband as I had been
about the wife. He had escaped my notice since our arrival,
but I had, as a much older man, met him . . . at some earlier
time. Like his wife, none the less, he had now struck me as

a stranger, and it was not till, in his room, I stood a little
face to face with him that I made out the wonderful reason
. . . that I was *not* a much older man. . . . It was he who was
old—it was he who was older" (21). But just as Gilbert Long
subscribed to the narrator's view at Paddington, so at Newmarch the artist Ford Obert, who has not known the Brissendens before, guilelessly corroborates the narrator's view by
exclaiming against the Brissendens' May-and-December marriage: "Why had so fine a young creature married a man three
times her age? He was of course astounded when I told him
the young creature was much nearer three times Brissenden's
(28). It is during this exchange, therefore, during his third
conversation with Obert at the end of the first day, that the
narrator feels impelled to form the theory that will dictate
his subsequent speculations. Just as Gilbert Long interpreted
the significance of the change in Mrs. Brissenden to the narrator at Paddington, so now the narrator in a similar relationship to Ford Obert proposes a fuller interpretation of the
implications of the phenomena he has observed.

He sees the case of the Brissendens as an extreme, "a fair,
though a gross, illustration of what almost always occur[s]"
(128) in a marriage between youth and age. Age grows
younger at the expense of youth. "There was really a touching truth in it, the stuff of . . . an apologue or a parable. 'One
of the pair,' I said, 'has to pay for the other. What ensues is a
miracle' " (29). In the specific instance " 'Mrs. Briss had
to get her new blood, her extra allowance of time and
bloom' " (29). These she has extracted from Guy, " 'and he
. . . to supply her, has had to tap the sacred fount. But the
sacred fount is like the greedy man's description of the turkey
as an "awkward" dinner dish. It may be sometimes too much
for a single share, but it's not enough to go round' " (29).
Obert asks, " 'So that, paying to his last drop, Mr. Briss, as

you call him, can only die of the business?' " " 'Oh, not yet, I hope. But before *her*—yes: long' " (29–30). The beneficiary, the narrator concludes, is selfishly unaware, but the " 'author of the sacrifice' " (30), whose motive is love, is conscious and therefore self-conscious with others.

Now the narrator has presented a fantastical hypothesis, the stuff of romance not reality, but he has prefaced his remarks to Obert with an observation that may easily reassure the reader: this is "the stuff of . . . an apologue or a parable." By putting these words into the narrator's account James allows for the extravagance of the hypothesis his character has proposed. So long as the narrator sees the stuff of which he speaks in a figurative or allegorical sense, the reader is not much disposed to try to discredit him. This implication of the good sense of the narrator is, of course, congenial with the impression of him that one has gradually formed throughout the first two chapters. He is an intelligent person, analytic by disposition, who has been drawn into an interest in a problem by other persons and by some strange observations of his own which have been corroborated by others. Now he is sufficiently beguiled, and sufficiently acute, to have become intensely interested in a perplexing series of phenomena. Nonetheless, his very choice of words, "anecdote," "riddle," "accidents," suggests the degree of his detachment. So do his low metaphors: even the possibility of Mrs. Brissenden's depleting the vital forces of her husband to the point of his dying prematurely, this narrator has tossed off with a reference to the old joke about the turkey. He registers his skepticism over Mrs. Briss's idea that Lady John supplies Gilbert Long with wit by asking if that operation is comparable to the administration of cod-liver oil, by the spoon or by the drop. What he has not observed he flatly rejects, for example Ford Obert's intuition that May Server is now strange to the point of being frightening. Thus far the narrator seems eminently level-headed, skeptical, not constitutionally given to wild flights of fancy, and not prone to take the present phenomena too seriously. He seems a highly credible witness.

This is exactly what James intended, I believe, both for the sake of verisimilitude in presenting a fantastical conception and for the sake of amusement in leading the reader into too easy a reliance upon the narrator's interpretations. The portrait of the narrator in the first two chapters appears to attest to his reliability, just as the sequence of interested or convinced narrators in *The Turn of the Screw* seems by implication to testify to the veracity of the experience recorded.[2] The twist that the reader should bear in mind, however, is that despite all the reserve and speculation that have characterized the narrator's attitude he has devised a set of hypotheses which he will use primarily to examine not the more credible, "fair though gross," case of the Brissendens but the far more incredible case of Gilbert Long and an unknown lady. He will devote most of his interest to the speculation that he has seemed to reject as far-fetched, to the theory that Gilbert Long's new brilliance is achieved at the expense of the wit of a woman in love with him; to the theory, in other words, that the stupid can grow clever. The reader therefore is launched, along with the narrator, into the purely imaginary. This is the point at which the adventure really begins.

Now (in Chapter III) it is the next morning. Fairly bursting with his theory, the narrator strikes up a conversation with Mrs. Brissenden on an allusion to their talk at Paddington yesterday. But, surprisingly, she "seemed not quite to remember where we had been" (32); he has to recall her speculation about Lady John to her. This momentary im-

---

[2] Cf. Edel, "An Introductory Essay," *The Sacred Fount*, pp. xxiv–xxv.

passe ought to forewarn the reader. Since the narrator is far
more involved in his idea than he can expect other persons to
be, from this point his remarks and speculations will be influenced by his conviction that a certain relationship must
exist. But other characters will answer him with reference
only to the "external appearance" of his conversation and to
the partial confidences which he bestows on them. In the
present scene, for example, Mrs. Brissenden has no knowledge of the hypotheses in relation to which the narrator is
pursuing his inquiry into the affairs of Gilbert Long, since
these hypotheses are based on his observations of her and her
husband. But she at least satisfies his conditions in that, as
beneficiary, she seems blandly unaware that she is not good
for her husband (42–3).

Gradually the narrator succeeds in talking Mrs. Briss
round to his view, and together they speculate on which
woman instead of Lady John might be the one. Mrs. Briss
obligingly nominates almost every woman at the house party
(39), but none quite fits the narrator's idea: "*Any* idiot
wouldn't be to the purpose. If it was enough that a woman
was a fool the search might become hopeless" (37). She suggests that perhaps the person is not at the house party, but he
patiently explains why according to his conviction she *must*
be here. At last, when they come upon Briss walking with May
Server, Mrs. Briss proposes the only woman that they hadn't
thought of: " 'May Server!' " (44) and the apparent avidity
of her speculation gives the narrator and the reader a momentary insight into the external appearance of his own
inquiries: "It was by her insistance [*sic*] . . . that my thought
was quickened. It even felt a kind of chill—an odd revulsion
—at the touch of her eagerness. Singular perhaps that only
then . . . the curiosity to which I had so freely surrendered
myself began to strike me as wanting in taste. It was reflected

in Mrs. Brissenden quite by my fault" (45). He concludes
with the observation that Mrs. Brissenden "put me off with
Guy, and I couldn't help feeling it as a sign of her concentra-
tion" (47).

Regarding the scene from outside the narrator's point of
view, one cannot help feeling that Mrs. Brissenden wanted to
get away from this assertive, insistent, and insatiably curious
person. For one thing, he has made her uncomfortable by
developing his theory about Long through an analogy with
what he considers her vampirish relationship to her husband.
Without knowing the narrator's assumptions about their
relationship, she might justly wonder what he was implying
by an observation such as " 'Well, at all events, you don't
separate. He doesn't really suffer you out of his sight, and . . .
you don't leave him at home.' " " 'Why shouldn't I?' she
asked, looking at me, I thought, just a trifle harder" (40).
Should she be afraid to leave her husband alone at home, and
if so why? Why shouldn't she leave him if she wants to do so?
What, after all, have she and Briss in common with " 'the
parties to an abandoned flirtation' "? (40) Hereafter she seems
to meet the narrator's observations with what he considers an
"odd mixture of the receptive and the derisive" (42).

Secondly, Mrs. Briss tries several times in this conversation
to tell the narrator without being rude that his own judgments are not necessarily those of everyone else. She thinks
more highly of women, for example, than he does, an attitude
hinted in her seeing more in Lady John's repartee, and in
both the choice of words ("admit," "prettily") and the substance of one of her observations: " 'I'm glad you admit, at
any rate,' she continued, 'that it does take what you so
prettily call some woman's secretly giving him of her best to
account for [Gilbert Long]' " (34). Of his view of Lady John,
Mrs. Briss remarks: " 'It proves nothing, you know, that *you*
don't like her.' " " 'No. It would prove more if she didn't like

me, which—fatuous fool as you may find me—I verily believe she does. If she hated me it would be, you see, for my ruthless analysis of her secret. She *has* no secret' " (34). Mrs. Briss presently asks if the narrator "then regarded Gilbert Long as now exalted to the position of the most brilliant of [their] companions. 'The cleverest man of the party?'—it pulled me up a little. 'Hardly that, perhaps—for don't you see the proofs I'm myself giving you? But say he *is*'—I considered— 'the cleverest but one.' The next moment I had seen what she meant. 'In that case the thing we're looking for ought logically to be the person, of the opposite sex, giving us the maximum sense of depletion for his benefit? The biggest fool, you suggest, *must,* consistently, be the right one?' " (37–8) Mrs. Briss has suggested nothing of the kind. The narrator has interpreted her question in the light of his theory, in which he has just been catechizing her. But a much more obvious meaning for her question would be, do you really think Gilbert Long is as brilliant as all that?

Finally, then, the narrator sometimes misses Mrs. Brissenden's point despite his acuity because he is too enamoured of his own point of view and too assured of the accuracy of his own judgments. He either overrules her, therefore, or sees in her remarks a reference to his own intelligence. Gilbert Long would certainly be the cleverest man at the party (in accordance with the narrator's theory) if the narrator were not forced in all humility to feel that he himself is. Lady John cannot be the woman in Gilbert Long's life because if she were she would hate the narrator for so shrewdly perceiving her secret, and instead she likes him. In this matter of the narrator's pride, however, Mrs. Brissenden is most gentle of all. She dismisses their disagreement over the degree of cleverness of Lady John, for example, with a passing compliment: " 'Oh, you've a standard of wit!' " (32)

Such are some of the negative qualities in the narrator

which may explain Mrs. Brissenden's ardent departure at the end of Chapter III to analyze May Server. He has a disconcerting habit of scrutinizing other persons and their relationships. He has overruled her whenever she has disagreed with him. And he is excessively proud. Both logical and perceptive herself, Mrs. Brissenden obviously admires his ingenuity, but she has not been spontaneously moved by his conviction so much as by his wit, and the reader need not mistake her acquiescence for unqualified acceptance of the narrator's views. Her apparent attitude at this point represents a comparatively objective reaction both to his character and to his theory. Meanwhile, her behavior has been appropriate either to a casual friend on a holiday weekend or to a lady, who is normally expected to be a gracious listener. She has sympathetically entered into the hunt on a rather pedestrian, gossipy level, though she is discreet.

The reader now has sufficient information about the narrator accurately to assess all his prior and subsequent inquiries. Since a continuous explication of his misguided adventure would run to a volume longer than the novel, however, let us focus on three significant sequences: Chapters I and II, which originally seemed so clearly to testify to the narrator's reliability; Chapters XII through XIV, which contain the concluding midnight colloquy between the narrator and Mrs. Brissenden; and Chapter VIII, in which all the ironies converge in a climactic interview between the narrator and May Server as they sit alone together in the wood. I shall try to show how the reader, in these sequences, generalizing from the insight into the narrator attained in Chapter III, may accurately evaluate his convictions and conclusions.

Beginning with a re-examination of the first two chapters, one can now see that the narrator's habit of scrutiny, and the intensity in general with which he pursues a subject in which he is interested, have thus far discomfited not only Mrs. Brissenden but everyone else with whom he has appeared. At Paddington, Gilbert Long had asked "why [the narrator] stared at him so hard" (7) and had supposed that the narrator was laughing at him: "He . . . more than suspected me, clever and critical as I was, of amusement at his artless prattle" (7). Later that afternoon the narrator suspected that his awareness that Gilbert Long had become a more accomplished conversationalist had also caught Lady John's attention: "[Long] was unconscious of how he had 'come out'—which was exactly what sharpened my wonder. Lady John, on her side, was thoroughly conscious, and I had a fancy that she looked at me to measure how far *I* was. I cared, naturally, not in the least what she guessed; her interest for me was all in the operation of her influence. I am afraid I watched to catch it in the act—watched her with a curiosity of which she might well have become aware" (16). Subsequently he recorded that just before dinner his friend Ford Obert "wanted to get off to dress, but I still held him" (20). After dinner the narrator realized that Briss had become aware that he was being scrutinized (23–4). Still later, in pressing an inquiry, he had again made Long uncomfortable: "Distinctly, he was uneasy —though as yet perhaps but vaguely—at what I might be coming to. That was precisely my idea, and if I pitied him a little for my pressure my idea was yet what most possessed me" (24). If, in short, other persons may withhold comments from the narrator in ensuing scenes, or even avoid him, the reason is simply that his habits of intense scrutiny and secretive inquiry make them reticent. They suspect that he knows more than they about the matter in hand or that they themselves are objects of his curiosity. They either fear what he may perceive or, believing that he perceives much, are deferential to his expressed views.

The narrator's tendency to ignore Mrs. Brissenden's opinions prompts the further insight that he has on the whole agreed with other characters thus far only because other characters have agreed with him. When a point of difference has arisen, he has overruled the other person. When he pressed Mrs. Brissenden, she acquiesced. When he pressed Long, Long became angry, and was suitably punished by the narrator's modifying his good opinion of him:

"Do you mean there's nothing in [Guy Brissenden] that strikes you?"

On this, unmistakably, he looked at me hard. " 'Strikes' me—in that boy? Nothing in him, that I know of, ever struck me in my life. He's not an object of the smallest interest to me!"

I felt that if I insisted I should really stir up the old Long, the stolid coxcomb, capable of rudeness, with whose redemption, re-absorption, supersession . . . I had been so happily impressed. "Oh, of course, if you haven't noticed, you haven't, and the matter I was going to speak of will have no point. You won't know what I mean." With which I paused long enough to let his curiosity operate if his denial had been sincere. But it hadn't.   (24–5)

So long, of course, as the narrator dismisses as insincere or implausible any view that runs counter to his own conviction, his theory will remain intact.

If disagreeing with the narrator makes Long again seem to be his old self, what made the narrator initially revise his estimate? May pride in his own judgment, or his good opinion of himself, have been a determinant in his formation of a favorable opinion of Long? That in fact proves to be true: the basis on which the narrator judged Gilbert Long stupid was that Gilbert Long ignored him between house parties at Newmarch. This time Long is more courteous, perhaps, rather than more intelligent, since they meet on their way back again to another house party at Newmarch. The reader

may legitimately speculate hereafter that the narrator's judgments are not wholly objective, but that they reflect in part
other people's respective attitudes or manner toward him.

Collectively, then, the case against the narrator in the first
three chapters may be summarized as follows: His hypothesis
about the Brissendens, the reader will concede, is "fair though
gross," perhaps extreme but not implausible. Ford Obert has
vouched for the narrator's view of the external appearance of
the couple. Yet there is little reason to question that a rather
grave (110) young man with bad posture (197) might age
prematurely; or that a woman married late in her thirties
to a man younger than herself—especially a woman as witty,
lively, and socially adept as Mrs. Brissenden has shown herself
to be—should prolong the effect of youthfulness. To Gilbert
Long's initial reaction to Mrs. Brissenden at Paddington, the
narrator had, as a matter of fact, opposed such a straightforward explanation: " 'What has happened to her is simply
that—well, that nothing has.' " " 'Nothing has happened?
But, my dear man, she has been married. That's supposed to
be something' " (6). Nor is there reason to question very
seriously the narrator's figurative explanation of this relationship as an instance of age sustaining itself on youth. When
one examines the relationship which the narrator would
interpret by analogy, however, one sees that his assumption
rests on far more tenuous grounds. Analogy, to begin with,
is not proof, yet the narrator's speculative intensity and assurance in Chapter III are not consistent with the seemingly
cautious attitude he displayed in the opening chapter, when
Mrs. Brissenden was celebrating the improvement in Long.
Secondly, the narrator's conviction that Long has undergone
an intellectual metamorphosis is never wholly endorsed by
another character, though it is for a time accepted by Mrs.
Brissenden. What Mrs. Brissenden spontaneously volunteered

at Paddington was that "she had never seen a man so improved" (8), an effect that might possibly proceed from
Long's being in love with anyone. What Ford Obert will say
in Chapter IV is not that Long is a gifted (52) or eloquent
(53) conversationalist, as the narrator proposes to himself
while he watches Obert and Long from across the picture
gallery, but that Long has said to him " 'characteristic
[things] . . . whimsical, fanciful, funny. . . . He talks to talk,
but he's really amusing' " (59). The reader cannot take the
remarks of either Mrs. Brissenden or Ford Obert, therefore,
as conclusive support of the narrator's assumption of a fundamental change in Long's intellectual capacity. That throws
one back on the narrator's own ground for forming the assumption: Gilbert Long was more courteous to him at the
railway station than he had usually been in the past. Surely
flimsy evidence.

For the present Mrs. Brissenden's explanation of the change
for the better in Long seems much more plausible: Gilbert
Long cares for Lady John. Lady John is " 'a very clever
woman,' " whose company is " 'a lift' " to others (9), and her
influence is what has improved Long: " 'It has positively
given him a mind and a tongue. . . . As they're known to be
always together, and she from morning till night as pointed
as a hat-pin, it proves just what one sees' " (10). This view of
Lady John's character, the reader finds, is re-enforced by the
narrator's own description of her, despite the fact that his
attitude is satiric: "She was pretty, prompt, hard, and, in a
way that was special to her, a mistress at once of 'culture' and
of slang. She was like a hat—with one of Mrs. Briss's hat-pins
—askew on the bust of Virgil. . . . [She] remained for each
. . . interlocutor as fresh as the clown bounding into the
ring" (17–8). Lady John is a "life of the party" type, brassy
perhaps, but someone who might stimulate lively response in
others.

Finally, then, the reader may distrust the narrator not only because he leans heavily on analogy as a basis for conviction; advances a theory that is not supported by other characters, themselves clever persons—because Newmarch courts the clever (37, 98); and forms his new estimate of Long on slight evidence, namely an instance of his being well mannered; but also because the narrator maintains a position that is logically suspect. He commits the fallacy of unnecessary complexity in an inductive inquiry, and it is legitimate to challenge him on this ground because he prides himself on his logic. In the present instance Mrs. Brissenden has proposed an interpretation of a given situation which is far simpler than the narrator's and which logically is to be preferred, therefore, unless he disproves it by introducing new facts. But he never does. It is Mrs. Brissenden herself who is at the end of the novel to produce what passes for a new fact, that her husband has discovered Lady John and Long in a compromising moment, which tips the scale in favor of her less ingenious but more plausible view.

If from this point in the novel (the end of Chapter III), the reader were to skip to the end of the book, he would see that Mrs. Brissenden's assault on the narrator's theory, supported by concessions the narrator himself makes, may finally be taken as just, although her motives may be suspect. All she does in that concluding interview is to assert certain limitations in him and weaknesses in his argument that the reader can discover for himself by a close reading of the opening chapters. The last four chapters, as a structural unit, counterbalance the first two, with the weights for and against the narrator's case redistributed. That is the structural significance, perhaps, of their falling on the third day, in the hours after midnight (200). On the first day (I–II), as we have seen, the emphasis is on the narrator's reliability, and except for a retrospective view after reading III the reader might easily overlook certain revealing particulars. On the second day (III–X) he records his adventure, and the reader must, for the most part, find his own way interpretively. On the third day (XI–XIV), however, the original balance is readjusted so that there is increasingly more reason to disbelieve the narrator and proportionately less that can be found to his credit. Obert in the end diverges by implication (XI), and Mrs. Brissenden, at last wishing to protect her own position more than she wishes to be agreeable, openly challenges him.

Mrs. Briss asserts that Long is " 'a prize fool' " (292), a view, of course, that had once been the narrator's own. When he bridles, she reminds him that he himself had flatly denied the possibility of a stupid man's becoming more intelligent:

"I thought that just what you told me, this morning or yesterday, was that you had never known a case of the conversion of an idiot."
. . . "It's true it would have been the only one."
"Ah, you'll have to do without it!"   (292–3)

Her reference goes back to Paddington Station and the narrator's own views at the time when he was made to appear to the reader most level-headed, cautious, and skeptical. Of course to deny a change in Long is, as the narrator himself acknowledges (262, 297), to attack his own theory at the root. If Long is not fundamentally changed, the narrator's own superstructure of thought to account for such a change must be erected on a false premise, and in the end he concedes that this is true (311).

Mrs. Brissenden, in affirming her conviction, muses: " 'But [Long's] perfectly stupid. I don't see how we can have fancied ——!' " (294) And that is another clue; there is no reason why the reader should have granted that Long was fundamentally changed, because the narrator never indicated a valid reason for thinking so. Mrs. Brissenden (though a self-interested motive may have made her willing to endorse a favorable change in Long), ostensibly yielded to the narrator's positiveness and his wit, not to any kind of factual demonstration. And this charge she also brings against him now: " 'With your art of putting things, one doesn't know where one is' " (262). " 'As soon as I was not with you—I mean with you personally—you *never* had my sympathy' " (287).

> "As soon as I was away from you I hated you."
> "Hated *me?*"
> "Well, hated . . . your theory." (288)

Ironically, the momentary conviction or interest he can arouse in others, and the consequent deference that they pay him, have constantly reassured and incited the narrator to further speculations at points when his sense of decorum might otherwise have made him hesitate. In Chapter IV Ford Obert encourages him, though at the end of the chapter Obert adopts an agnostic attitude toward the whole inquiry which he disclaims only belatedly (in XI). In Chapter V Mrs. Brissenden apparently succumbs. In VII Guy Brissenden mistakenly believes that the narrator knows more than he himself does about May Server. Here is the first reason, then, why the narrator has persisted so far in his own delusion; the deference of others has ministered to his pride, and his pride, in turn, has encouraged him to value his own opinions over those of others. Mrs. Brissenden now for the first time explicitly indicates that she is also aware of this habit in the narrator:

> "I didn't suppose," said Mrs. Briss, "that you'd like it. I didn't suppose that you'd accept it or even listen to it. But I owed it to you——" She hesitated.

"You owed it to me to let me know what you thought of me
even should it prove very disagreeable?"
      . . . "I owed it to myself."   (279–80)

The second reason that the narrator has been able to persist
in his delusion and, therefore, in the elaboration of his ex-
travagant theory, is that those persons who may wish to preserve their privacy, shying away from his scrutiny, have not
hampered him with further facts about themselves, as I shall
illustrate in a moment. And, finally, his own reticence has
complemented their reserve. The reason the narrator himself
has intermittently proposed for asking no leading questions
of others is that he wishes to preserve the privacy of those
whom he scrutinizes from the gaze of other persons potentially less discreet than himself. If the reader desires another
reason, Guy Brissenden has proposed it: " 'If you've kept
them off, it must be because you differ with them' " (116).
Both the charge that he is not in the confidence of others and
the admission that he has not solicited their views also come
out in this final conversation with Mrs. Brissenden (as she
speaks in favor of her own view):

"Oh, but add to my impression everyone else's impression! Has
anyone noticed anything?"
"Ah, I don't know what anyone has noticed. I haven't," I
brooded, "ventured—as you know—-to ask anyone."
"Well, if you had you'd have seen—seen, I mean, all they don't
see. If they had been conscious they'd have talked."
I thought. "To me?"
"Well, I'm not sure to you; people have such a notion of what
you embroider on things that they're rather afraid to commit
themselves or to lead you on."   (298)

Hence, both immune to the disagreement of others and
isolated from their confidence, the narrator has gradually

assigned imagined reasons for appearances that have more obvious explanations to a person better informed. Mrs. Brissenden challenges him on this limitation as well:

> "How do you know what I mayn't, or may, have liked?"
> It did bring me to. "Because you were conscious of not telling me? Well, even if you didn't——!"
> "That made no difference," she inquired with a generous derision, "because you could always imagine? Of course you could always imagine—which is precisely what is the matter with you! But I'm surprised at your coming to me with it once more as evidence of anything." (313; cf. 101)

Mrs. Briss is herself as perceptive of significant details and as logical as the narrator and yet has the added advantages of being less proud, more tactful, and far more subtle. She therefore enjoys a greater degree of the confidence of others: " 'It's to *me* they might have spoken—or to each other' " (300). Her consequent extensive knowledge of the social scene is, like every other significant detail, indicated in the opening pages (4) and acknowledged by the narrator himself at the end (305). And one of the crowning ironies of the novel is simply that Mrs. Brissenden emerges in this interview as the person the narrator had believed himself to be.

Unfortunately, the concluding chapters are not so clear as the above excerpts would imply, for their constructional method is that of the novel as a whole at its most complex. To arrive at a straightforward interpretation, the reader must first recognize two superficial sources of confusion. To do so he should be guided by the admonitions implanted throughout the text and, most frequently, at the beginnings of chapters or in the interior monologues of the narrator. One such passage appears near the beginning of Chapter XII, just before Mrs. Briss and the narrator begin to speak:

More extraordinary perhaps than anything else, moreover, was just my perception of [a flaw in Mrs. Briss's confidence]; which gives the value of all that each of us so visibly felt the other to have put together, to have been making out and gathering in, since we parted. . . . We *had,* of a truth, arrived at our results—though mine were naturally the ones for me to believe in; and it was prodigious that we openely [sic] met not at all where we had last left each other, but exactly on what our subsequent suppressed processes had achieved.   (243)

And there is a reminder in Chapter XIII:

It could *not* but be exciting to talk, as we talked, on the basis of those suppressed processes and unavowed references which made the meaning of our meeting so different from its form. We knew ourselves—what moved me, that is, was that she knew me—to mean, at every point, immensely more than I said or than she answered; just as she saw me, at the same points, measure the space by which her answers fell short.   (272)

Ironically, this second passage is commonly cited by exasperated readers as an indication of James's unintelligibility, while in fact it is a key to one origin of the reader's difficulty. The narrator is pointing out in the first quotation that his own and Mrs. Brissenden's assumptions may differ, since the two have not talked together since noon. In the second he is hinting that the meaning of their highly allusive conversation is affected by their respective assumptions. In other words the reader must reflect on what each of the speakers must believe, and suppose the other to believe, in order to grasp the whole sense of their dialogue. This principle holds true for the book as a whole.

One difficulty in this instance is a misconception of Mrs. Brissenden's in which the narrator encourages her. Though he often verbally dismisses the opinions of others, keeping all the lead strings in his own hand, he nevertheless incorporates into his own subsequent thinking whatever part of their opinions will nurture his own convictions. Hence in the first chapter he laughed at Mrs. Briss's explanation that Lady John has given Gilbert Long " 'a mind and a tongue' " (10) and yet in Chapter III depended on her acknowledgment of improvement in Long to support his own theory. Similarly, at the end of Chapter III he utterly refused to accept her nomination of May Server as the unknown lady whose intellect supplied Gilbert Long and yet in Chapter IV he wholeheartedly pursued the theory that May Server might be the lady in question. By evening he feels certain that she is (154).

Having consistently been subject to the narrator's point of view, the reader may have forgotten that the narrator has never admitted to Mrs. Brissenden his adoption of her nominee as the lady whom he seeks. In a word he lightly warns the reader that he does not intend to do so now: "I had promised her, on my honour, to be candid, but even if I were disposed to cease to contest her identification of Mrs. Server. . . ." (237) That is a primary source of superficial confusion in this interview. For in returning to her original proposition at the end, that Lady John, not Mrs. Server, is the person involved with Gilbert Long (251, 303), Mrs. Briss believes that she is agreeing with the narrator, while in fact she is toppling his whole theory. Hence he presses her to extract from her a reason why he should reject May Server, while outwardly professing the conviction that Mrs. Brissenden believes he holds, that May Server is not the woman. Fully half of the verbal sparring in these last three chapters depends on this difference in the preconceptions of the two speakers. In Chapter XIII alone the narrator rephrases his question—Why did you change your mind?—at least a dozen times.

Like Mrs. Brissenden, the narrator labors under a misconception that obfuscates the obvious in this conversation, but
his is self-imposed. His misconception is nothing less than the
theory he has developed to get at the truth. Originally he had
assumed an affinity between Brissenden and Mrs. Server based
on their common plight as victims. But earlier this same
evening, when Mrs. Brissenden and Gilbert Long appeared
together for the first time since their arrival at Newmarch
(180–81), it occurred to him that the vampires might also have
developed a mutual consciousness, perhaps as a result of what
he now considers his own almost providential awareness:
"Mrs. Brissenden and Long had been hitherto magnificently
without it [i.e., without a recognition of the nature of their
effect on their respective victims], and I was responsible perhaps for having, in a mood practically much stupider than the
stupidest of theirs, put them gratuitously and helplessly *on* it.
To be without it was the most consistent, the most successful,
because the most amiable, form of selfishness; and why should
people admirably equipped for remaining so . . . be made to
begin to vibrate, to crack and split, from within?" (183–4)
He reasons, therefore, that Mrs. Brissenden's desire to have
this midnight tête-à-tête with him is a countermove by the
vampires, and he assesses her present outspoken and tenacious
resistance to his further inquiry as a frightened attempt to
keep the victims from getting away:

They both had their treasure to guard, and they had looked to
each other with the instinct of help. They had felt, on either side,
the victim possibly slip, and they had connected the possibility
with an interest discernibly inspired in me by this personage, and
with a relation discoverably established by that interest. It
wouldn't have been a danger, perhaps, if the two victims hadn't

slipped together. . . . How could they know, Gilbert Long and Mrs. Briss, that actively to communicate a consciousness to my other friends [the victims] had no part in my plan? (274)

But here again, if the reader assumes a more objective point of view than that of the narrator, he can find a more obvious explanation of Mrs. Brissenden's behavior. For she was initially pleased at the narrator's acknowledgment of improvement in Gilbert Long, and explained that this must indicate the influence of a clever woman (page 40, above). She betrayed hardness when the narrator brought their conversation round to her relationship with Briss (page 46). She has persistently been willing to help the narrator find another woman involved with Gilbert Long. She has summoned the narrator to this interview at a very irregular hour, and she did so after she had observed him contemplating her and Gilbert Long. Now, during their conversation, the narrator discerns a perceptible flaw in her confidence, and she makes an impassioned effort to thwart him in any further inquiry by denying his basic premises. All these facts of course suggest that she herself is the woman involved with Long. And Mrs. Brissenden must believe that the narrator is on the point of discovering this fact simply because he has not admitted that his candidate is Mrs. Server. Gilbert Long's behavior also bears out this interpretation. He, too, betrays pleasure at the improvement in the opposite member of the presumptive liaison (page 40, above). He is overtly critical of Brissenden, whom he considers dull: " 'She [Grace] has been married so little and so stupidly' " (6; cf. 24). And he, like Mrs. Brissenden, reveals discomfiture under scrutiny (page 49, above). Hence the symptoms which the narrator has observed, Brissenden's general decline and Mrs. Brissenden's and Gilbert Long's new lease on life, may all proceed from the most obvious and pedestrian causes.[3]

The theory that the narrator develops and celebrates as a means of approaching the truth consistently stands between him and that truth. Above all, this ironic principle dominates the climactic interview in the wood with Mrs. Server (in Chapter VIII), but a full appreciation of that interview must be retrospective. Only after the reader has sufficient accrued evidence against the narrator to dare not to weigh his testimony seriously can he savor the high comedy implicit in that scene. For it is not enough that the narrator should fail to discover the woman who has metamorphosed Long. He himself is the man for whom he seeks, the person whose presence accounts for May Server's strange behavior. That is why the narrator meets Mrs. Brissenden's final assertion—that May Server " 'couldn't be gone' " mentally because she has been flirting with Guy Brissenden—with a "queer grimace" and "a chill to [his] mind" (316–7). And I believe it is why James allows his characters, in a book so intricately constructed, to return in the last five pages to the question of May Server. James is inviting the reader to consider the narrator's own stake in the social situation.

By the beginning of Chapter VIII one already knows a great deal about the narrator's preferences in people, notably in women. Lady John he does not like because she is so blatant that she leaves no room for his imagination (17) and because she rivals him. She can sit quietly with such a person as Guy Brissenden but feels obliged to "be clever" with the narrator (101–2); her characteristic response to his wit

[3] I am indebted to Mr. Cargill's essay on *The Sacred Fount* in developing my case against Mrs. Brissenden. See pp. 293–294 of his *Novels of Henry James* for further support of the conclusion that she is having an affair with Gilbert Long.

is to match him joke for joke, and that is irritating (17–8,
102). Mrs. Brissenden he likes and admires because she
is both attractive and clever. She is intelligent enough to
appreciate his keen observation and his nuance (or, from her
point of view, his lively but potentially dangerous repartee),
yet she is normally inclined to defer to him conversationally.
She is a touchstone for his wit, and he allows for wit in her by
seeing her as an "apt pupil" (35). But Mrs. Server is the one
for whom he has the tenderest feeling, the one whom he consistently wishes to assist or protect. May Server is the most
womanly of the three according to a conventional standard.
The qualities in her which the narrator perpetually remarks
are her beauty and her charm. Her conversation is neither
hard and bright like Lady John's nor informed by logic like
Mrs. Brissenden's, but rather disorganized, "a little scattered
and troubled" (49). She herself is "a little helpless and vague"
(18). She does what the narrator wishes her to do, not moving
across the gallery till he gives her leave (50, 52). She is deferential to every male; in the gallery she asks the opinion of
each of the three men present (55–6). When she listens to
Gilbert Long she looks over at Obert and the narrator "as if to
intimate with her shining, lingering eyes that [they] wouldn't
be surprised at her transports if [they] suspected what her
entertainer, whom she had never known for such a humourist,
was saying" (59–60). When she sits with the narrator in the
wood her conversation consists primarily of a sequence of
questions that set up his remarks, together with a compliment,
" 'I think you're very kind' " (135), and a tacit plea for
assistance: " 'Do you mean—a—do you mean——?' With
which she broke off on a small weak titter and a still weaker
exclamation. 'There are so *many* gentlemen!' " (143) May
Server is, in short, the helpless type, and she knows exactly
how to appeal to a man of the narrator's pride and volubility,

and, for that matter, to most other men. Small wonder Mrs. Brissenden in an off moment calls her horrid (316).[4]

That Mrs. Server succeeds in interesting the narrator is implied from a number of quarters. Both Mrs. Brissenden and Ford Obert have reserved the privilege of watching him as he watches others (76, 219), and their intimations on this point happen strangely to agree. Mrs. Brissenden explicitly asks him if he is falling in love with May Server (72), and Ford Obert explains to him in the gallery that the discomfort he feels—a "nervousness" which the narrator himself records for the reader's benefit (60)—is the effect of Mrs. Server's behavior: " 'Do you remember what I said to you about her yesterday afternoon? She darts from flower to flower, but she clings, for the time, to each. You've been feeling, I judge, the force of my remark' " (61). What Obert had suggested earlier was simply that Mrs. Server's notable behavior has been occasioned by a change in her own circumstances. When he painted her portrait, he explains, " 'her affections were not then, I imagine, at her disposal. I judge that that's what it must have been. They were fixed—with intensity; and it made the difference with *me*. Her imagination had, for the time, rested its wing. At present it's ready for flight—it seeks a fresh perch. It's trying. Take care' " (19–20).[5] As for Lady John's pedestrian speculations along the same line, the narrator hardly deigns to put them on record (180, 185–6). But he himself speculates whether he might be in love: "Had I my-

---

[4] The parallel classification of the men in the narrator's view is: Guy Brissenden (whom he pities), Ford Obert (whose views he respects), and Gilbert Long (who does not rise to the narrator's particular brand of wit and whom he therefore dislikes).

[5] Obert's remark, together with the fact that she is alone at the house party and has apparently come to other Newmarch parties alone (14), is the reader's ground for assuming that Mrs. Server is a widow, or perhaps divorced.

self suddenly fallen so much in love with Mrs. Server that the care for her reputation had become with me an obsession? It was of no use saying I simply pitied her" (60–61; cf. 93–5).[6] In one of the most detachedly retrospective passages in the book he acknowledges his subsequent inability to forget her (197).

That May Server in her turn has singled out the narrator is implied by Ford Obert's injunction, " 'Look for the last man. . . . I daresay it would be he' " (69), interpreted in the light of Mrs. Brissenden's explanation of the reason that Mrs. Server pays court to practically every man at the party: " 'The logic is simply that she has a terror of appearing to encourage anyone in particular' " (79; cf. 64). Since it is only the narrator whom she obviously and consistently avoids (113–4), the implication is that it is he whom she is trying to win. Further, Guy Brissenden, who sees more of Mrs. Server than any other person during this week end, takes for granted a connection between her struggle to keep up appearances and her suspicion that the narrator knows what is wrong with her (114–5, 119).

What defeats May Server is the narrator's omnipresent theory, for by the time that he meets her in the wood (VIII) he is so assured of its verity, recently encouraged by the deference of Obert (IV), Mrs. Briss (V), and Guy Brissenden (VII), that he can only conclude that she is in love with Gilbert Long (137, 154). Hence, though he describes this interview as

---

[6] The narrator frequently employs this technique in his memoir, that of raising the point that a detached critic of his own interpretations might in a given instance raise against him. The effect of his habit is to give him the appearance of being reasonable, but as a consequence he is later able to palm off his own view on the unwary. Though in the present instance, for example, "pity" does not seem to the narrator to be an adequate expression of his feeling, it is precisely the concept he will reintroduce at the time of the climactic interview (107, 136, 153).

a kind of magic hour, and comes close to admitting his love—
" 'I've . . . been in love for a whole [day]' " (149)—he concludes by entrusting May to Guy Brissenden, whose company,
according to the theory, must bring greater solace than that
of anyone else: the "victims" have an affinity based on their
common fate. They have, indeed, but their bond appears to
be simply that each of them loves another person too much
for comfort.

Mrs. Briss is patently indifferent toward Briss much of the
time (40–41, 43). The narrator underscores the point:

"[Mrs. Server] may have a sympathy."
. . . "You mean she may be sorry for him? On what ground?"
. . . "You neglect him so!"   (76–7)

So does Lady John: " 'She has him so in hand that they're
neither of them in as much danger as would count for a
mouse. It doesn't prevent his liking to dally by the way—for
she dallies by the way, and he does everything she does.
Haven't I observed her,' Lady John continued, 'dallying a
little, so far as that goes, with *you?*' " (176) Lady John's assumption also reveals the external appearance of Mrs. Briss's
prolonged tête-à-tête with the narrator and suggests why
Briss, in delivering his wife's unusual request that the narrator see her again after midnight, may not be very happy;
hence the symptoms in him which the narrator records. Mrs.
Brissenden's indifference is what consumes her husband,
whether or not he may specifically know about the relationship with Long.

Presumably the analogy that holds Ford Obert's attention
all day, the analogy which has brought him to believe that
May is in love with the narrator and the narrator, possibly,
in love with May—Obert is still making up his mind in

Chapter XI—is this one: Briss obviously adores his wife; Mrs. Briss is off talking to the narrator. May Server constantly flits to Briss for company; in whom else may she have an interest? Perhaps in the narrator:

"What I call the light of day [says Obert] is the sense I've arrived at of [May's] vision."

"Her vision?" . . .

"Of what [she and Briss] have in common. *His*—poor chap's —extraordinary situation too."

"Bravo! And you see in that——?"

"What, all these hours, has touched, fascinated, drawn her. It has been an instinct with her."

"Bravissimo!"

. . . "The instinct of sympathy, pity—the response to fellowship in misery; the sight of another fate as strange, as monstrous as her own." (223–4)

Here Obert is supplying the only insight that Mrs. Brissenden, in Chapters XII through XIV, is not in a position to offer, that the relationship Mrs. Server shares with Briss need not be "making love" (316) but an affinity based on a common plight, that, presumably, of a one-sided love for another person.

The particular ravage that the narrator notes in Mrs. Server in the wood, therefore, need not be attributed to a disintegrating mind so much as to her confusion at the combination of tenderness and apparent disinterest the narrator manifests toward her, together with her disappointment, perhaps, at not bagging him. Guy Brissenden has provided enough information about Mrs. Server to suggest that she may be seeking security as well as affection in a new match: " 'She *isn't* happy. . . . Her circumstances are nothing wonderful. She has none too much money; she has had three children and lost them; and nobody that belongs to her appears ever to have been particularly nice to her' " (119). By evening, however, she has recovered (212 ff.), for as Obert explains, " 'A woman's lover doesn't matter—doesn't matter at least to anyone but himself . . . when once she has given him up' " (221). The narrator's belated recognition of what has happened to him is the crowning note on which the novel ends, though the reader can hardly blame the poor man for not being explicit about his enlightenment.

Read in this way, *The Sacred Fount* is high comedy wonderfully sustained. The narrator, with his head perpetually in a theoretic, psychologic cloud, commits some remarkable *faux pas,* asking Lady John if it really is true that she has such a " 'fund of indulgence' " for Gilbert Long as everybody supposes (178), and Mrs. Briss if she inquired of Long himself who the lady is (263). There are innumerable particular ironies. Interpreted in this way the book, though oversubtle (a "profitless labyrinth"), emerges as the *"jeu d'esprit"* and "consistent joke" that James claimed it was in replying to Mrs. Humphry Ward's inquiry about his intention. It has, as he claimed, "and applied quite rigorously and constructively, . . . its own little law of composition." [7] *The Sacred Fount* read from this perspective also moves quickly, at a pace in keeping with its tenuity and its comic tone.

[7] These passages, except the first, are from an unpublished letter to Mrs. Ward cited by Leon Edel in his "Introductory Essay" to the Grove Press edition of *The Sacred Fount* (p. xxx), from which I quote. "Profitless labyrinth," quoted from the same source *(loc. cit.),* occurs in an unpublished letter to the Duchess of Sutherland.

CHAPTER 3

The Figurative Debacle

IT is surprising, in view of the scrutiny to which *The Sacred Fount* has been subjected in recent years, that no inclusive or systematic study of its figurative language has been ventured. This is part of a larger issue, for, although the importance of figurative language in James's fiction is widely acknowledged, the very pervasiveness of metaphor in his later writing makes it hard to arrive at conclusive statements about his usage generally, and even a particular text may present a formidable amount of metaphorical detail to be accounted for. Only recently a first major effort has been made in this direction by Robert L. Gale, who in *The Caught Image* attempts to deal with the imagery in all of James's novels and stories. The primary value of Mr. Gale's book, as he himself indicates, is that it alerts the general reader to the importance of metaphor in James's fiction and provides a wealth of "evidence" for more specialized studies—especially, I might add, for comparative studies of similar figures occurring in separate volumes. It is not especially helpful, however, in dealing with problems of interpretation within a specific text, because the images have lost their contexts and because Mr. Gale's interpretive remarks, though sometimes provocative, are very sketchy, as I will illustrate later in this chapter.

In specific studies of *The Sacred Fount* few writers have
dealt very seriously with imagery. Arnold P. Hinchliffe's remarks hardly require extended answer. The incompleteness
of such a statement as this one, for example, will become
clearer as we proceed: "The images, however, fall under two
significant headings. First, there is the recurrent flower image
which receives its finest expression when May Server is observed at the piano [p. 167]. Second, there are the images of
violence. All the women are constantly under arms; and the
poor discovered woman stifles shrieks and gasps, while the
narrator's own prose style is described as explosive." [1] James
Reaney's method of indulging in free associations seems to me
wholly unreliable and one by which the reader may potentially conclude anything he wishes. In arguing that the book
dignifies the narrator as a prototype of the artist, or of humanity, striving to know, he writes:

There are other images that further support the dignity of the
theme we have outlined. The title itself belongs to the legendary
world of magic fountains and wells of life. Mr. Edel shows us how
the myth of Egeria and King Numa has relevance here; May
Server is Gilbert Long's Egeria. The story's country house also
becomes a "castle of enchantment" in whose park wanders the
bewitched and exhausted May Server. As the narrator comes upon
Mrs. Server in the park he feels as if he were "stalking a fawn"—
an image from the world of Malory. Ford Obert, the painter, says
to the narrator: "I've blown on my torch . . . till . . . it has guided
me, through a magnificent chiaroscuro of colour and shadow, out
into the light of day" (222). Both these last images of hunt and
cave appear, by the way, in *The Republic* and are august symbols
of man's search for reality. The narrator sees the whole "civilized
state" of the society in which he lives as a "concentric series of

[1] "Henry James's *The Sacred Fount,*" *Texas Studies in Literature and
Language,* II (Spring 1960), 91–92.

circles of rose-colour . . . for the so salient little figure of Mrs. Server" (167). Dante's paradisal rose comes to mind with Mrs. Server as a pastel and pathetic Beatrice. . . . It is, of course, with a great deal of irony that these legendary images are used.[2]

But mightn't these images, in the hands of Mr. Geismar, for instance, prove entirely different things? And does anyone really believe that James is here evoking Malory or Plato or Beatrice? He was perhaps saying that the narrator is soft on Mrs. Server and that he therefore sneaks up on her and looks at her through rose-colored glasses. As for the flaming torch, it is Obert who brandishes it, and not this supposed proto-type. The all-important issue is surely *context* in dealing with James's figures, which very commonly show a close relation-ship to germinal ideas, or which have specialized meanings that derive from the interaction of characters in specific dramatic situations. Hence Maisie uses metaphors involving games and toys because these are the stuff of a child's experi-ence and vocabulary. And the golden bowl, intrinsically nothing remarkable, becomes fraught with meaning when we consider the terrific irony of Charlotte's offering it to Maggie Verver. When James makes allusions as such, he usually quotes directly, or identifies his subject by name, as he does with Egeria, or in some way calls attention to the fact that a cross-reference is being invoked.

The one person who seems to me to have posed a very compelling interpretation of *The Sacred Fount* taking into consideration the effect of James's figures upon its tone is Sidney Finkelstein. In general, Mr. Finkelstein conceives of the development of the novel as a three-act drama, in which the narrator, successively appearing in the roles of observer,

---

[2] "The Condition of Light: Henry James's *The Sacred Fount,*" *University of Toronto Quarterly,* XXXI (January 1962), 141.

sympathizer, and conscience, is at first fascinated by his observations, then appalled at Mrs. Server's manifest sufferings,
and at last morally indignant at Mrs. Brissenden's vampirism
(as defined by his theory) in their concluding dialogue. The
"tone" of Act I, which includes the early dialogues with Mrs.
Brissenden and other persons, is "light and witty." [3] "Deeply
felt imagery with tragic overtones, expressing the emotional
involvement of the narrator, characterizes all of Act II," [4]
which focuses on Mrs. Server. And the "new tone" of Act III,
which treats the last scene between the narrator and Mrs.
Brissenden, "is that of 'difficult' Henry James conversation
carried to its limits. . . . The added note is that of deception." [5] Mr. Finkelstein then concludes (in part) that on the
grounds of character development and tone *The Sacred
Fount* cannot plausibly be placed within the sphere of
comedy:

> The view of *The Sacred Fount* as a satiric comedy, whose butt
> is the narrator, clashes with the style of the book. James in his
> comic mode, as in the short stories "The Real Thing" and "The
> Figure in the Carpet," more or less abandons the creation of char-
> acter in terms of complex consciousness with refinements of inner
> conflict. The characters are sharply outlined, unproblematical,
> almost "types." In the dialogue there is little fencing with words
> or matching of states of awareness, but rather clarity and sparkle.
> The narrator, if there is one, is also a "type," from whom James
> unambiguously detaches himself. . . .
>   These stories, fair examples of James's style of comedy, are
> opposite in manner and tone to *The Sacred Fount,* which has all
> the characteristics of the straightforward, serious or tragic James
> style. If at the outset, when the narrator is a detached observer of
> his fellow guests, the tone is that of light comedy, it soon changes,

[3] "The 'Mystery' of Henry James's *The Sacred Fount*," p. 759.
[4] *Ibid.*, p. 760.   [5] *Ibid.*, p. 763.

to be replaced by the poignant, engaged imagery of the passages that have been previously quoted, such as those describing Mrs. Server. Other images evoke the anguish beneath the brave appearance. James speaks of the "deadly little ache of her heroic grin," of how she "folded up her manner in her flounced parasol, which she seemed to drag after her as a sorry soldier his musket," of the "absolute wreck of her storm," of her sensibility "waving from the mast, with a bravery that went to the heart, the last tatter of its flag." This imagery, which gives the novel its high poetic quality, is the narrator's imagery, and it is not the kind that James at any time puts into the mouth of a buffoon, a fool, a self-deluding snooper, of anyone he wishes to satirize.[6]

The question of characterization I will return to in Chapter 6, but briefly the answer to Mr. Finkelstein is, I think, that this narrator does begin as a type character just as the novel begins as a short story and a joke. But as James's idea gradually took form, so his characterization of the narrator became more complicated, the story longer, and its tone increasingly ambiguous.[7] Turning, then, to Mr. Finkelstein's argument about tone, one might first ask how he himself would account for James's having written a three-act drama which is first light and witty, then tragic, and finally a conversational *pièce de résistance* spiced by duplicity on the one hand and moral indignation on the other. But the problem does not arise in his argument because he sees the figurative evidence which he amasses chiefly with reference to "Act II"—May Server's Act, with its center in the scene in the wood—as a conclusive indication that the narrator is exempt from satire. Why not generalize from the beginning or the end of the book instead?

In fact, I believe, what we have here is a manifestation of one of the subtler effects of that "incomplete fusion" of two

---

[6] *Ibid.*, pp. 767, 768–769.   [7] See pp. 155–162, below.

subjects which I noted in Chapter I as a major hazard for the reader of *The Sacred Fount*.[8] The tone of the book is inconsistent because the language that naturally pertains to Mrs. Server's and Brissenden's dilemmas, and that which pertains to the narrator's character and quest are on the whole mutually antagonistic, and James sometimes contemplates the effects of vampirism, and at other times the self-delusion of the narrator. Of course James also had a practical, and no doubt thoroughly conscious, reason for allowing the narrator to speak with such intensity of May Server's sufferings. For he had to communicate indirectly the idea that the narrator was in love with May Server, and one way in which he did so was to allow the narrator to translate love into the terms of pity, as I observed in Chapter II.[9] This would be my answer to Mr. Finkelstein as to why James might allow his narrator to speak so movingly while yet considering him fair game for satire. James must have supposed that the effect of these descriptions would be modified for his reader because the reader had meanwhile come to terms with the narrator. Hence they become simply one more ironic illustration of how deluded the narrator can be. In any case, we need not assume that the sufferings of Mrs. Server are so acute as the narrator portrays them, because we remember that this interpretation depends on our believing that the process of disintegration which he agonizingly details actually occurs. But of course it does not, and objectively observed Mrs. Server looks much more durable than the narrator's descriptions of her admit. In short, the reader must allow, as always, for the subjectivity of the character in forming a reaction to his descriptions of suffering. We can form a fairer estimate of the total effect of figurative language in the book than that Mr. Finkelstein urges upon us if we will differentiate the objects

[8] See pp. 15–18, above.   [9] See pp. 64–65, above.

of the figures in given instances. How do the narrator and his quest fare metaphorically, for instance? Or Mrs. Server herself in the dropped comments of other characters? These are the questions which I will pose in this chapter, and then presently I will return to more somber figures in considering the serious aspects of the novel in Chapter 5.

At the outset the narrator describes himself as a man for whom "the vision of life is an obsession" (23), one whose inquiry is leading into "the mystery of mysteries," into "the power not one's self, in the given instance, that made for passion" (17). Such an inquiry is a profound one, and the narrator takes it seriously, inaugurating several recurrent metaphors to characterize the kind of relationship he contemplates. Its inequality might be expressed, for example, in monetary terms: " 'One of the pair . . . has to pay for the other. What ensues is a miracle, and miracles are expensive' " (29). He reapplies this figure when he and Mrs. Brissenden come unexpectedly upon Briss and Mrs. Server for the first time: "There would have been a pertinence . . . in this juxtaposition of the two persons who paid . . . so heroically" (45). He reasons out a successive stage of his theory in such terms. May it be that the gift of intellect or of vitality made by one person to another grows in the giving? "It was as if these elements might really multiply in the transfer made of them; as if the borrower practically found himself—or herself—in possession of a greater sum than the known property of the creditor" (53). In a more sinister vein the narrator conceives of the opposites in an unequal relationship as agents (31, 274) and victims (30, 43, 234) of a sacrifice. By the end of the second day, as he contemplates Briss and Mrs. Server in evening dress, he sees them almost as chosen victims: "They had truly been arrayed and anointed, they had truly been isolated, for their sacrifice" (168–9). Finally, the narrator adopts a metaphor fatal in its implications, that of the sacred fount: the more devoted person in such a relationship may be expected to overtax his own vitality to satisfy the demands of his opposite (29, 38, 47, 198).

The narrator takes seriously not only the phenomena he is examining but also his own role as interpreter of them. He insistently reiterates that his interest in the couples is theoretic and not personal. He wishes to discover a principle, "a law that would fit, that would strike [him] as governing the delicate phenomena" (23), not to expose or embarrass individuals. To define his detached role and perspective, he introduces yet other serious imagistic motifs. The social panorama before him and its implications form a "picture" (10) continuously enriched by "fresh accessions" (13) and so vivid to his sense that he can imagine it at times as literally hanging before him (84, 174). When he argues with Mrs. Brissenden, it is "as if [he] had hung the picture before her, so that she had fairly to look at it" (285). At other times he sees the persons he examines as forming a "little gallery," a "small collection," "the museum of those who put to [him] with such intensity the question of what had happened to them" (22). He imagines that he perceives Lady John's "emotions, and what determined them, as behind clear glass" (102), as if they were items in his museum; and he describes various other observed particulars as "fit[ting] so completely to the other pieces in [his] collection" (104) or as "playing a part in [his] exhibition" (183). Thirdly, he considers the whole episode he records a "tense little drama" for which the hours at Newmarch are the stage (48; cf. 138), finally anticipating the denouement in such terms: "every actor in the play that had so unexpectedly insisted on constituting itself for me sat forth as with an intimation that they were not to be so easily disposed of. It was as if there were some last act to be performed before the curtain could fall. Would the definite dramatic signal for ringing the curtain down be then only—as a grand climax and *coup de théâtre*—the due attestation that poor Briss had succumbed to inexorable time and Mrs. Server given way under a cerebral lesion?" (168)

All six of these metaphorical motifs—those of paying, sacrifice, and the sacred fount; the drama, the collection, and the picture—are notable for their serious tone, especially the first three. And the latter three are notable also for the consistency with which they reaffirm the narrator's self-appointed role as an observer and interpreter of the action rather than a participant in it. Judging by these figures, one might tentatively conclude that the narrator is both dignified and detached despite his excessive self-confidence; that his inquiry is essentially serious despite the fact that, pursued in a given social context, it may have comic or pedestrian implications. If these inductions were true, however, why should the narrator at times speak of the pursuit of his inquiry as a kind of game? Why should he sometimes describe himself in terms that would better suit Fido on the chase than a dignified, detached observer? "I felt from the first that if I was on the scent of something ultimate I had better waste neither my wonder nor my wisdom. I *was* on the scent—that I was sure of" (22–3). One hardly pursues the ultimate by olfactory means. Subsequently, the narrator makes out points " 'only after a hunt' " (42), till he feels that he is "on the track of a discovery" (59). Then, happily imagining that Ford Obert is going off on a "false scent" (65), the narrator agrees with his friend to proceed independently of one another: " 'Very good,' I returned, 'though I didn't in the least mean to set you digging so hard. However, dig on your side, by all means, while I dig on mine' " (65). Hereafter he noses about (65), covers his tracks (67), pricks up his ears (176); resisting the imputation that he is "prowling about" in search of Briss (109) but meanwhile admitting to himself that he has become "attached, morally, to [his] prey" (93) in the person of Mrs. Server: "While I moved a few steps toward her I felt almost as noiseless and guarded as if I were trapping a bird or stalking a fawn" (130). Figures suggesting animal-like characteristics in the narrator recur throughout the book. The final disgrace is being properly disciplined by Mrs. Brissenden: "It was as if she had decided . . . just to rub my nose into what I had been spelling out" (302). This figure indicates how far the two have come since morning, when Mrs. Briss felt that the narrator had performed the same service for her (70).

Such figures, needless to say, go far in undermining the narrator's gravity. They are reminiscent of the animal figures of *In the Cage,* which remind one that the telegraphist's insights are, after all, of a low order despite her acumen.[10] Similar figures may invite the reader also to consider what the narrator and Mrs. Server have in common. Why should she, birdlike to the narrator (133, 150), a little fawn (130), seem to Mrs. Briss to be " 'on the pounce' " (75; cf. 83, 167); seem to Ford Obert to be capable of "prowling" about the house after midnight in search of the narrator? (206; cf. 246). Are the narrator and Mrs. Server a pair, perhaps, she on the prowl in the social scene as he is in the theoretic? Is she unexceptional except in the narrator's view of her? And if so, may that imply the state of his affections?

The "games" figures resemble the hunting metaphor in functions. If the narrator's inquiry is to be taken as seriously as he invites, why should he continually characterize it as a

___

[10] For a discussion of the animal figures of *In the Cage,* see my article "James's *In the Cage:* An Approach through the Figurative Language," *University of Toronto Quarterly,* XXXI (January 1962), 173–174.

sort of social game (66, 68), a kind of "high sport" (164), like hide-and-seek (37) or tug of war (256–7), carried on "for [his] private amusement"? (40; cf. 291) "I could toss the ball myself, I could catch it and send it back, and familiarity had now made this exercise—in my own inner precincts—easy and safe" (174). The most telling figures of this group occur when he is with Lady John. Both suddenly see a meaning in the uncommon juxtaposition of Mrs. Brissenden and Gilbert Long, and as a consequence both make a "dash" from "opposite ends" of a metaphorical field (185). In this moment of recognition Lady John is apparently reflecting upon the degree of intimacy between Mrs. Briss and Long, while the narrator first speculates that the "vampires" may have, by the agency of his own perceptiveness, been somehow put into relation with one another:

So much, at least, I saw Lady John as seeing, and my vision may be taken as representing the dash I have confessed myself as making from my end of our field. It offers us, to be exact, as jostling each other just sensibly—though *I* only might feel the bruise—in our business of picking up straws. Our view of the improved acquaintance was only a straw, but as I stooped to it I felt my head bump with my neighbour's. This might have made me ashamed of my eagerness, but, oddly enough, that effect was not to come. I felt in fact that, since we had even pulled against each other at the straw, I carried off, in turning away, the larger piece.   (188)

Picking up straws in hot rivalry with Lady John, whom he considers a fool ("a hat . . . askew on the bust of Virgil") is not a very dignified occupation for the narrator. Such a figure consequently points up the tremendous distance between his theoretical statements of the nature of his inquiry and his practical pursuit of it. Such an image also poses the question whether he and Lady John may not have more in common than the narrator would care to admit. In short, the "games" figures, like the recurrent hunting metaphor, are comic in tone and therefore connotatively oppose those figures that dignify the narrator and his search.

While certain figures belie the narrator's dignity and seriousness of purpose, others call into question his detachment. Though the narrator begins as an observer, he gradually wishes to become a prime mover, one capable of altering the course of events by sheer force of insight. This idea first begins to occur to him as he privately celebrates what he believes to be his exceptional insight into the true state of Lady John's and Gilbert Long's feelings toward one another: "To see all this was at the time, I remember, to be as inhumanly amused as if one had found one could create something. I had created nothing but a clue or two to the larger comprehension I still needed, yet I positively found myself overtaken by a mild artistic glow" (104). Presently the narrator takes for granted that in his insight into May Server he possesses a " 'supernatural acuteness' " (125). He fancies that he exercises some control over her movements when she appears in the wood: "It was exactly as if she had been there by the operation of my intelligence, or even by that . . . of my feeling" (129). To exercise such a "providential supervision" over Mrs. Server, the narrator must eventually conclude, is in turn to become "morally responsible, so to speak, for her" (154), and in time he embraces the other victim, Brissenden, in his benevolence. When Briss turns away abruptly from Lady John, leaving her on the narrator's hands, the latter can only conclude that "he had begun . . . to depend upon me, that I already in a fashion figured to him—and on amazingly little evidence after all—as his natural protector, his providence, his effective omniscience. Like Mrs. Server herself, he was materially on my hands" (170–71). They become "conjoined in [his] charity" (274).

His theory has become for the narrator not a hypothesis to be tested at every step but a "creation" and a "vision" (174): "the sense thus established of my superior vision may perfectly have gone a little to my head. If it was a frenzied fallacy I was all to blame, but if it was anything else whatever it was naturally intoxicating" (177). "*I* alone was magnificently and absurdly aware—everyone else was benightedly out of it" (177). In such a state of mind the narrator is of course impervious to such a warning as Lady John offers in passing: " 'give up, for a quiet life, the attempt to be a providence. You can't be a providence and not be a bore. A real providence *knows;* whereas you . . . have to find out—and to find out even by asking "the likes of" *me*' " (176). But the reader should take such a warning to heart, for if the narrator's theory has become to him that creation of intellect by which he judges himself superior to others, almost godlike, one may expect that he will be more concerned with the preservation of that theory than with testing it objectively. It is the reader himself who must be detached.

In summary, both the narrator's character and his objectivity are called into question by inconsistencies among the groups of figures characterizing him and his attitude toward his inquiry, and from the moment that the reader perceives this kind of discrepancy in the novel he has one key to its interpretation on the social level. If the narrator is not consistent, the reader is not obligated to accept his word consistently. Viewing the narrator more critically, then, one will find that again and again figurative motifs testify to his limited insight, to his lack of progress in the pursuit of his inquiry, and, ultimately, to his defeat at the hands of Mrs. Brissenden.

There is the turned back, for instance. In the course of the novel every other major figure is represented at some point as having his back turned toward the narrator. This

specific might easily pass as a descriptive detail in given contexts if it were not for two attendant facts, one of them that
the backs are sometimes turned in self-protection or dismissal.
When after dinner the first evening the narrator goads Gilbert Long to scrutinize Briss, "as if to examine a picture
behind him, the personage in question suddenly turned his
back" (26). Similarly, Long, manifesting discomfort in relation to the narrator during the discussion before the mysterious portrait, turns away from the group (58). On the second
evening Mrs. Brissenden's "handsome affirmative back" (192)
testifies to an attitude she will later define, in effect, as one
of temporary dismissal (244). Secondly, although other characters may turn away from him, the narrator is undeterred
because he considers backs almost as informative as faces;
backs may indicate what he feels sure the persons' faces
would indicate if he could see them. He is not abashed, therefore, when Brissenden turns away that first evening, because
"The poor youth's back, before [him and Long], still as if
consciously presented, confessed to the burden of time" (27).
It does not perturb him to recognize later that he "seemed
perpetually, at Newmarch, to be taking [Brissenden's] measure from behind" (227), because after all "it was when [Bris-
senden] showed you, from behind, the singular stoop of his
shoulders, that he looked oldest" (197). Gilbert Long's back
is "replete . . . with a guilty significance" (38) when the narrator believes that he and Mrs. Brissenden have caught Long
with the unidentified woman, and Mrs. Brissenden's own
"handsome affirmative back" the narrator understands as
testifying to her defiance at his tacit recognition of her real
age: "Didn't what I saw strike me as saying straight *at* me,
as far as possible, 'I *am* young—I am and I *will* be; see, *see*
if I'm not; there, there, there!' . . . If her face had not been
hidden, should I not precisely have found myself right in

believing that it looked, exactly, for those instants, dreadfully older than it had ever yet had to? The answer ideally cynical would have been: 'Oh, any woman of your resources can look young with her back turned! But you've had to turn it to make that proclamation' " (194). The fact is, however, that Mrs. Brissenden, both at Paddington and in the final scene, alludes to her age without any apparent embarrassment (8–9, 245), though she is understandably responsive to the narrator's intermittent compliments on her youthful appearance. Hence this particular motif suggests both that the narrator is not in the confidence of others and that he may at times overinterpret the slight data at his disposal. This motif raises the question, in other words, of whether his insight may not be limited. It symbolizes that isolation from other characters which eventually leads him into theoretic excess. And it exemplifies the fact that the reader of James, if he will visualize any given scene, may attain an insight from the physical attitudes of the characters.

Meanwhile, if the narrator's methods are inadequate, certain light images, those in which light is equated with insight, suggest that his results may also leave something to be desired. The narrator admittedly begins, of course, with a riddle, which he proposes to solve by analogy. With Mrs. Briss he begins by "raking the gloom for lights" (37). " 'I start,' " he tells Obert, " 'in the dark—or in a darkness lighted, at best, by what you have called the torch of my analogy' " (66). The interesting thing, however, is that the light of insight in the narrator is never quite divorced in subsequent figures from the idea of gloom or darkness. His insights are seemingly modified by partial failures of insight, while imagistically both Obert and Mrs. Briss move on from darkness into light.

In the two scenes in which Obert momentarily allows himself to become involved he is characterized as a source of light. His mention that the portrait's face resembles someone at the party is "illuminating" to the narrator (57); his attention focused on May is, to the narrator's view, a kind of "searchlight" (61). Furthermore, in Obert's hand the narrator's hypothesis " 'sheds a great light' " (63), is " 'a torch in the darkness' " (64). The only problem, as far as the narrator is concerned, is that he himself doesn't know what the torch of his analogy has led Obert to discover: "He didn't say what [his own idea] was, and I didn't ask, intimating thereby that I held it to be in this manner we were playing the game" (68). For the present the narrator succeeds in discouraging Obert's further inquiries: "After an instant the light went out of his face" (69). But by that evening, acknowledging again " 'the touch of [the narrator's] analogy' " (216), Obert proclaims triumphantly that May Server has given up her lover: " 'You gave me the pieces. I've but put them together. You gave me the Brissendens—bound hand and foot; and I've but made them, in that sorry state, pull me through. I've blown on my torch, in other words, till, flaring and smoking, it has guided me, through a magnificent chiaroscuro of colour and shadow, out into the light of day' " (222). The light of day, he explains, is " 'the sense I've arrived at of [May's] vision . . . Of what [she and Briss] have in common' " (223).[11] In such figures it is Obert, not the narrator, who seems most able to use the narrator's analogy to stimulate insight, and the narrator himself is by Chapter XI reduced to such pitiful tactics as pleading, " 'You tell me [what you know] . . . first' " (223), while dangling before Obert the promise of greater confidences to come: " 'Oh, don't be afraid—[I have found] greater things than yours!' " (223)

It is Mrs. Brissenden whom the light images most distin-

[11] The nature of Obert's insight is discussed on pp. 66–67, above.

guish. She gives the narrator usable insights just as he provided Fort Obert with one. During their final interview he remarks this relationship, alluding to their conversations of the morning: " 'Even fighting was working, for we struck, you'll remember, sparks, and sparks were what we wanted. . . . Sparks are what we still want, and you've not come to me, I trust, with a mere spent match. I depend upon it that you've another to strike' " (257). The significant point about this metaphor is that Mrs. Briss brings fire, and the narrator, only a striking surface against which her wit may ignite. This relationship continues in the final interview. She "luminously" reminds him that his scrutiny has sometimes debarred him from the confidences of others (298). Her explanation that May Server wasn't all gone because she made love to Briss, the narrator must concede, "in fact brought light" (317). The narrator meanwhile keeps wavering between insight and confusion: " 'Light or darkness, my imagination rides me' " (276). "She was all logic now, and I could easily see, between my light and my darkness, how she would remain so" (304). In the end he willingly succumbs to darkness, however, for in order to preserve his own view of May Server, he must reject the final flash generated by his and Mrs. Brissenden's opposing views: "I felt [Mrs. Briss's] dreadful logic, but I couldn't—with my exquisite image all contrasted, as in a flash from flint, with this monstrosity—so much as entertain her question" (317). Mrs. Brissenden now withdraws "through the lighted rooms" (318), a descriptive image which should itself arrest the reader's attention, for the brilliance of the light in these hours past midnight has likewise been emphasized through recurrence in the last chapters of the novel. "In conformity with the large allowances of every sort that were the law of Newmarch, [the empty rooms] were still open and lighted" (207). After midnight the servants did not arrive to extinguish the lights, as the narrator expected (207), simply because Mrs. Briss had indicated, in anticipation of this interview, that she wished to sit up (241). Hence the stage for their meeting is "a desert on which the sun had still not set" (236), and the reader may ask himself whether Mrs. Brissenden's command of light and both her appearance and departure at moments when the narrator comments on the brightness of the light, may not symbolize her lucidity. It is her argument, and not the narrator's, which is most to be trusted at the end, for symbolically she brings light.[12]

If the reader still has reservations, he can turn, at last, to the building figures. The narrator has conceived of the gradual augmenting of his theory as the fashioning of a beautiful building. He begins with the simple activity of fitting pieces together: "It appeared then that the more things I fitted together the larger sense . . . they made" (127–8). Presently he emerges with "an airy structure" of hypotheses (144) in which he takes great pride: "I had puzzled out everything and put everything together; I was as morally confident and as intellectually triumphant as I have frankly here described myself" (142). Now the narrator aspires to an "ideal symmetry" (169), a "full roundness of [his] theory" (181), as his objective. Of course there are dangers implicit in such a quest: "These opposed couples balanced like bronze groups

---

[12] The longest interpretative statement on the imagery of *The Sacred Fount* which Robert L. Gale includes in *The Caught Image* deals with these light images, and I quote it here in full: "Characters in James who seek knowledge are frequently imaged as seeking light, flame, fire. Undoubtedly the most dogged and ingenious such seeker in all literature is the unnamed narrator of *The Sacred Fount,* which is adazzle with torches, blazes, flickering flames, flaring fires, and simple struck sparks. But that narrator, whose pleasures evidently are all intellectual, does not trouble himself with any emotional heat." (*The Caught Image* [Chapel Hill, N.C., 1964], p. 169.) Then follows a partial list of the figures cited above.

at the two ends of a chimney-piece, and the most I could say to myself in lucid deprecation of my thought was that I mustn't take them equally for granted merely *because* they balanced. Things in the real had a way of not balancing; it was all an affair, this fine symmetry, of artificial proportion" (182–3). But he is not deterred by this insight from proceeding to the erection, by midnight, of "a great glittering crystal palace" of thought (205). The narrator has erected an impressive structure. But there is a significant issue to be resolved, and it arises in the final interview with Mrs. Brissenden: however beautiful or perfect a building may be, it stands or falls depending on the strength of its foundation. The narrator's building rests on two fundamental assumptions, that Mrs. Server has become inane and Gilbert Long more intelligent, and these are precisely the assumptions that Mrs. Brissenden challenges. Hence the " 'perfect palace of thought' " (311) comes "rattling down" (310–11) in the end despite the perfect fitting of its parts:

"I seem myself to see [my "quite sublime structure"] again, perfect in every part," I pursued, "even while I thus speak to you, and to feel afresh that, weren't [*sic;* were it not for/?] the wretched accident of its weak foundation, it wouldn't have the shadow of a flaw. I've spoken of it in my conceivable regret . . . as already a mere heap of disfigured fragments; but that was the extravagance of my vexation, my despair. It's in point of fact so beautifully fitted that it comes apart piece by piece. . . . I should almost like, piece by piece, to hand them back to you." And this time I completed my figure. "I believe that . . . you'd find yourself placing them by your own sense in their order and rearing once more the splendid pile. Will you take just *one* of them from me again . . . ? She had remained silent, as if really in the presence of the rising magnificence of my metaphor, and it was not too late for the one chance left me."   (311–2)

But Mrs. Brissenden desists, and the narrator is left, as he says, in a "smash" (318).

Though the reader might plausibly question any one of these figurative debacles on the ground that the narrator constantly modifies his admissions of defeat with statements that throw the honesty of his interlocutors into question, yet the collective weight of the figurative language is oppressive. Here is a man who sniffs out and burrows for the ultimate; who refers to a question of life and death as if it were a game; a man who believes himself omniscient and everyone else "benightedly out of it." This investigator is one on whom others turn their backs, one who moves between darkness and light, one who erects a theory on weak foundations —a character, in short, who is the last person in the book whom the reader need take at his word. On what grounds could the reader possibly take seriously a person so characterized, however seriously that person may take himself?

James achieved both suspense and psychological verisimilitude by consistently working through his character's mind, but at the expense of clarity, since the narrator neither understands wholly nor can be expected willingly to reveal his own position. To some extent Mrs. Brissenden is a Jamesian *ficelle* whose function is to help the reader by articulating arguments against the narrator's imperfect methods, but she is not altogether reliable because of her own self-interest. In addition to Mrs. Brissenden's logic and the miscellaneous insights rendered through other characters less highly developed, James offers his reader at least two other, more subtle, sources of insight: first, this burden of ludicrous figures. For incongruities in James's figurative language may ever be taken as a source of insight, as here they constantly point toward the fundamental inconsistency between the narrator's self-portrait and a more objective view, and imply an imperfect integration of disparate subjects. Secondly, a provocative topical allusion, directly interpolated by James himself into one of the narrator's self-congratulatory rhapsodies, hints at the limitations of the character and may even imply a devastating judgment upon him. Let us turn, then, to this allusion in an attempt to rediscover the implications that it must have had for James at the end of the nineteenth century.

CHAPTER 4

The Exclusive Wagnerite

THE allusive passage occurs during those heady moments when the narrator yields both detachment and compassion in order to celebrate his own solitary intellectual mastery of the affairs of the two couples: "And I could only say to myself that this was the price—the price of the secret success, the lonely liberty and the intellectual joy. There were things that for so private and splendid a revel—that of the exclusive king with his Wagner opera—I could only let go, and the special torment of my case was that the condition of light, of the satisfaction of curiosity and of the attestation of triumph, was in this direct way the sacrifice of feeling" (296). Whether James was making an incidental remark or whether he was attempting to guide his reader at a crucial moment, his mention of "the exclusive king" is very strategically placed. For it occurs late in the final scene, when the divergence between the narrator and Mrs. Brissenden is greatest and the reader hardest pressed to arbitrate between their views. And it tips the scale, if not for Mrs. Brissenden, at least against the narrator. It may also be significant in assessing the argument that *The Sacred Fount* embodies a serious statement about the functioning of the artist. Variations on this idea, which is both current and pervasive, constitute the largest single body of opinion as to what *The Sacred Fount* is about. Yet no critic who holds this view has ever discussed the possible relevance of a passage which seems to me crucial in assessing its likelihood. This specific problem of interpretation in turn gives rise to a larger question, that of how pertinent seemingly casual allusions may be to the interpretation of James's fiction more generally. And, finally, the passage is intrinsically interesting as one in a sustained sequence of allusions in James's fiction which indicate that he, like so many of his contemporary English novelists, was susceptible to the profound imaginative impact of the Wagner movement.

"The exclusive king with his Wagner opera" is an appropriate description of Ludwig II of Bavaria, who reigned from 1864 to 1886. Throughout his reign Ludwig was the devoted patron of Wagner. His personal attachment for Wagner was so great that he was publicly attacked in the contemporary German press for his extravagance in supporting the composer and his schemes, while Wagner was suspected of exerting political influence on the king. Ludwig's personal idiosyncrasies included dressing himself as Tristan, Parsifal, or Lohengrin. He had a pond built in the Winter Garden at the top of the Royal Palace in Munich and there, dressed as "the Knight of the Swan," he would embark in a skiff "made after the pattern of the one in which Lohengrin appears drawn by the swan. . . . In this costume he was rowed about all through the night, while different coloured lamps and torches lit up the scene, also feather fans made the air cool, and soft music discoursed behind the thick curtains of foliage." [1] In 1874 Ludwig signed a financial guarantee to assist Wagner in building the festival opera house at Bayreuth for the production of the Ring.

[1] Frances Gerard, *The Romance of Ludwig II. of Bavaria* (London, 1899), pp. 160–161; 162, n. 1.

Ludwig II was an "exclusive king" because, over a period of years, he progressively debarred other persons from his presence, turning night into day and pursuing a variety of solitary nocturnal diversions. From 1870 he ceased attending public performances at the Court Theater in Munich and announced that "henceforward there would be private representations at the Court Theatre, the expense of which he would bear and of which he would be the sole spectator. . . ." [2] These private theatricals began at eleven or twelve at night, after the public theater had closed, and included plays especially written or produced for the occasion and also Wagnerian operas. After 1876 the king failed to appear at Court balls or entertainments.[3] Toward the end of 1884, "he allowed only four people to his intimate friendship. . . . He took to consulting spiritualists for the purpose of conversing with his departed friend [Wagner]. Rappings went on constantly, and Marie Antoinette and Louis XIV occasionally joined in the conversation." [4] By 1886 "the only communication he would hold with his Ministry was carried on through his hairdresser. Later he wished to be altogether alone and shut himself up in his bedchamber, commanding his bodyservants to stand outside his door to receive his commands. They were to signify their comprehension of the latter by scratching on the door panel." [5] Ludwig II was declared insane in June 1886, and efforts to depose him ended in his mysterious death by drowning.

Ludwig's elaborate solitary theatricals including Wagnerian operas and his celebrated patronage of Wagner seem clearly to identify him as the person alluded to by the narrator of *The Sacred Fount:* "for so private and splendid a revel—that of the exclusive king with his Wagner opera. . . ."

---

[2] *Ibid.,* p. 175.   [3] *Ibid.,* p. 233.
[4] *Ibid.,* p. 251.   [5] *Ibid.,* p. 258.

But the full implications of this allusion for the interpretation of the novel depend on a third aspect of Ludwig's biography: above all else he is known for his mania for building.
He built and furnished three castles, all of them located in
remote settings. Neuschwanstein, in the mountains of Bavaria, is decorated with heroes and heroines of the Nibelun-
genlied, as well as portraits of Louis XIV and Louis XV and
a bust of Marie Antoinette, whom Ludwig venerated. "Her
marble presentment stood next to his bed, so placed that his
eyes might fall upon her face when he awoke." [6] Linderhof,
a little "copy of the Trianon" furnished in the styles of Louis
XIV and Louis XV, is remarkable for having ten reception
rooms and only one bedroom, not to mention its artificial
grotto of Capri, made of cement and brown linen.[7] The
largest, most magnificent, and most inaccessible palace is the
unfinished Herrenchiemsee, an imitation of Versailles built
on the island of Herrenwörth. "When Ludwig was alone
[here] he indulged himself to the full in his eccentricities.
No one dared look at him; he would spend the night either
on the lake or in the hall of mirrors, where the thirty-three
chandeliers were all ablaze till long past midnight. . . . On
the occasion of these visits he was generally seized with some
idea for improving different portions of the building." [8]
Ludwig died in 1886 with plans already completed for con-
structing yet another castle, but he had been increasingly
thwarted by lack of funds. His first English biographer quotes
a desperate letter to the Court furrier written by the king
in behalf of this project only a month before his death:
"Speak to Ziegler. . . . Tell him that building is the only joy
of my life, and that since all my work has been so shamefully
stopped I am miserable. All day long I think of nothing but

---

[6] *Ibid.,* p. 196.   [7] *Ibid.,* pp. 197–201, *passim.*
[8] *Ibid.,* pp. 214–215.

abdication, suicide: the situation is intolerable; it must end. The building of my castles *must* proceed, and that will give me new life." [9]

The resemblance of Ludwig's passion to erect great buildings to that of the fictional character to build a " 'perfect palace of thought' " is obvious. This resemblance provides the reader with yet another reason for comparing the fictional narrator with the real king. Further, if James's narrator is to be compared with the Bavarian king, the implication is that his "private revel" is that of a madman and his palace of thought, however ingenious, the product of a mad fancy. Like Ludwig, he dwells within his palace in solitude; it has practical existence only for himself. Like Ludwig, he is (in Mrs. Brissenden's phrase) " 'an intelligent man gone wrong,' " a proud and inventive man who has a compulsion to build in order to fulfill, realize, and gratify himself. The apparent effect of the allusion—occurring as it does during these crucial moments of the final scene—is to suggest to the reader that the narrator's views need not be taken as a rational explanation of the affairs of other characters in the novel. And Mrs. Brissenden, however reprehensible she may be in her relationship with her husband, represents some sort of norm.

Yet, this inference about the quality of the narrator's argument need not rule out the possibility that his palace of thought is to be understood as having a viable life of its own. Ludwig's palaces still stand despite their wild origins. And might not the narrator's palace of thought exist as a work of art exists, irrespective of whether it corresponds to literal fact? Critics have often speculated that the novel represents some kind of symbolic statement about the artist. In answering Wilson's Follett's description of the book as a stupendous

[9] From a letter "Amongst the official documents" of Bavaria, quoted and translated by Miss Gerard, p. 294.

self-parody, for example, Mr. Edel writes: "Henry James's point in *The Sacred Fount* is not . . . that 'life' destroys the artist's 'make-believe,' but that the 'make-believe' has a reality of its own." [10] The question, then, is whether one can perhaps take Ludwig as a serious figure, as a type of the artist, as well as a humorous figure. If so, what may this imply about the narrator of *The Sacred Fount*? In order to assess what connotations James may have been summoning up in making such an allusion, let us look more closely at the popular image of Ludwig in England at the end of the nineteenth century.

The portrait of the king as I have presented it thus far is taken from the first English biography, *The Romance of Ludwig II. of Bavaria,* by Frances A. Gerard, published in London in September 1899, and in New York in October of that year. This book is decidedly "popular" in character. Miss Gerard is a conscientious and sympathetic biographer, but not an incisive one, and she quotes heavily from contemporary accounts of Ludwig. Her story is based principally on German sources, including personal memoirs, letters, and Bavarian state documents, which were generally publicized only after Ludwig's deposition, and also on English and American periodical and newspaper articles. In addition to Miss Gerard's biography and a flurry of reviews of it, at least twenty articles about Ludwig II appeared in England and America between 1873 and the publication of *The Sacred Fount* early in 1901.[11] A number of these must have come to James's attention, because they appeared in leading literary periodicals and sometimes in periodicals to which he himself

[10] Leon Edel, "An Introductory Essay," p. vi.
[11] See the Bibliography for a record of those articles that I know to exist. There are probably others, since much of this periodical literature is not indexed and the scope of my examination has been limited to the most likely sources. My objective here is of course to demonstrate the pervasiveness of the Ludwig material rather than to offer an exhaustive bibliography.

contributed during the nineties.[12] The Bavarian king attracted general notice outside of Germany for several reasons. His personal idiosyncrasies progressively attracted attention in a ruling monarch. His early espousal of Wagner's "music of the future" involved him in an European *cause célèbre.* And the dramatic episode of his deposition and presumptive suicide brought forth information previously suppressed in Germany. Ludwig's palaces were opened to the public in July 1886, and became a tourist attraction, especially perhaps in 1890 and 1900, when the Oberammergau Festival occurred. And finally, the triumph of the Wagner movement in England in the 1890's, together with the violent deaths at the end of the century of two great ladies closely identified with him, also recalled Ludwig II to memory.

The earliest English accounts of Ludwig II which I have located have no single objective beyond that of portraying or assessing him as a monarch. But Ludwig's idiosyncrasies are a recurrent theme in these pieces, and his relationship with Wagner also comes in for comment. The authors variously take a sentimental or a satiric view. "E.E.," for example, writing in *Lippincott's Magazine* in October 1873, maintains that the king is a man much misunderstood and slandered, and therefore sets out "to correct . . . the false impressions which have so long prevailed" [13] by demonstrating that Ludwig is a studious, pure, and serious-minded youth faithful to his kingly obligations. The writer must admit that "unfortunately, the king soon gave his people a plausible excuse for fault-finding by the unbounded favor which he bestowed upon Wagner, whose ideas and whose music were at that

[12] The latter include the *Atlantic Monthly, Harper's Monthly Magazine, Literature, The Speaker,* and *Temple Bar.*

[13] E. E., "The King of Bavaria," *Lippincott's Magazine,* XII (October 1873), 410.

time alike obnoxious to the majority of Germans." [14] But he concludes: "It may be that in the far-off future, long after the titles and prerogatives of royalty shall have been done away with and wellnigh forgotten, the virtues of this king, who is so poorly appreciated by his contemporaries, will be commemorated in some beautiful legend, like that of his favorite story of the Swan-Knight; since even now, when that chaste hero appears in the dazzling purity of his enchanted armor upon the Munich stage, one turns involuntarily to recognize his counterpart in the solitary occupant of the royal box." [15]

This is the sentimental view. Mark Twain, on the other hand, playfully satirizes the king's solitary theatricals in *A Tramp Abroad* (1880) under the title "An Eccentric King":

The King was sole audience. The opera proceeded, it was a piece with a storm in it; the mimic thunder began to mutter, the mimic wind began to wail and sough, and the mimic rain to patter. The King's interest rose higher and higher; it developed into enthusiasm. He cried out,—

"It is good, very good indeed! But I will have real rain! Turn on the water [the sprinkler system for fire]!" . . .

The thunder boomed, the lightning glared, the storm-winds raged, the deluge poured down. The mimic royalty on the stage, with their soaked satins clinging to their bodies, slopped around ankle deep in water, warbling their sweetest and best, the fiddlers under the eaves of the stage sawed away for dear life, with the cold overflow spouting down the backs of their necks, and the dry and happy King sat in his lofty box and wore his gloves to ribbons applauding.[16]

The virulent antithesis to E.E.'s sentimentality, however, is

---

[14] *Loc. cit.*   [15] *Ibid.,* p. 415.
[16] Mark Twain (Samuel L. Clemens), *A Tramp Abroad* (Hartford and London, 1880), pp. 97–98.

provided by E. Reclus in a two-part article which appeared in the *Galaxy* in April and May, 1875. Reclus berates Ludwig for political ineptitude and indifference, for preferring music to affairs of state.[17] He berates the Germans for mistaking "cretinism" for "innocence" and "insanity for a state of grace." [18] He implies a homosexual tendency in Ludwig.[19] He judges him a would-be artist over whom the egocentric, immoral Wagner could exercise an excessive influence because of the king's susceptible temper: " 'I do not make verses; it is true I cannot rhyme, but I feel poetry; I am a living poem. . . . If I am not yet a genius, I have the spirit of genius; I am a potential genius! . . . I am a Wagner, for I am Wagnerian!' " [20] Reclus enumerates the absurdities of Ludwig's palace of Hohenschwangen,[21] he finds fault with Ludwig's predilection for solitude and the solitary theatricals,[22] and finally dismisses him as "being virtuoso only by half.[23] Among negative assessments, this one is most vitriolic, but the specific charges of abnormal behavior, self-indulgence, and Wagnerism are ones that consistently recur hereafter, with differing degrees of allowance made for the king. The two basic attitudes represented by Reclus and E.E., satiric and apologetic, also persist.

After June 1886, the idea of madness is inseparable from the public image of Ludwig II. For his peculiarities, as well as the medical diagnosis of his condition, were widely publicized by his ministers at the time of his deposition to exonerate themselves from questionable motives in dealing with a monarch who was liked by the Bavarian peasantry.[24] Lud-

[17] E. Reclus, "Louis II. of Bavaria. Or, Romanticism on the Throne," [Part I], *The Galaxy*, XIX (April 1875), 528.

[18] *Loc. cit.*   [19] *Ibid.*, p. 533.

[20] *Ibid.*, [Part II], *The Galaxy*, XIX (May 1875), 605; cf. 608.

[21] *Ibid.*, pp. 608–609.   [22] *Ibid.*, pp. 610–611.   [23] *Ibid.*, p. 613.

[24] See the London *Times*, "The Late King of Bavaria," June 17, 1886, p. 5, and "Bavaria," June 19, 1886, p. 7.

wig's story was a major news item in England for two weeks as more and more information was made public. The deposition was announced in the *Times* on June 11:

By the statemen of Munich the greatest efforts have been made to avert the disaster that has now happened, and even the Bavarian Press . . . did its best to hush up the scandal, telling the outer world as little as possible of the King's eccentric habits—of his passion for constituting himself the sole audience at theatrical performances, of his boundless and indiscriminate prodigality, of his mania for expending fabulous sums in the building of new and fantastic palaces, and of his lavish patronage of particular arts—though to this latter foible of His Majesty Germany owes the happy nurture of the genius of one of her greatest sons, as well as the splendid temple of his worship at Bayreuth.[25]

On June 12 a *Times* correspondent added: "The mental aberration of the King is now described as having reached a climax, or, in other words, culminated in raving madness." [26] After the king's presumptive suicide occurred on June 14, the medical opinion that had been determined June 8 and that had led to his deposition was also published in the *Times*. This report designates Ludwig as having paranoia.[27] Thereafter Ludwig's insanity was constantly reiterated in the press, and physical aspects of his condition were specified. From Berlin June 16: "The King's brain showed decided signs of disease and degeneration in various forms.[28] From Munich June 18: "Dr. Von Schleiss, surgeon in ordinary to the late King . . . now . . . states that the chronic inflammation

[25] "Proclamation of a Regency in Bavaria," London *Times*, June 11, 1886, p. 5.

[26] "Bavaria," London *Times*, June 12, 1886, p. 7.

[27] "Suicide of the King of Bavaria," London *Times*, June 15, 1886, p. 3.

[28] "The Late King of Bavaria," London *Times*, June 16, 1886, p. 5.

of the cerebral membrane, which was disclosed by the post mortem examination, justifies in his opinion the theory of insanity." [29]

Repercussions of these events are apparent in periodical literature throughout the summer of 1886 and into the autumn. In England the *Illustrated London News* and the *Graphic* both gave substantial coverage to the king's funeral.[30] An article dealing with Lugwig II appeared in the *Spectator* on June 19 and two in the *Saturday Review* on the same day, followed by others in *Temple Bar* and the *Contemporary Review* in August.[31] In America *Littell's Living Age* reprinted four of these pieces. On July 17 *Harper's Weekly* carried an illustrated article on the Wittelsbachs, borrowing pictures from the English graphics; and the *Critic* published "Ludwig's Fitting End," gleaned from the *Pall Mall Gazette,* on the third of July.[32] In October both the

[29] "The Late King of Bavaria," London *Times,* June 18, 1886, p. 5.

[30] "The Late King of Bavaria," *Illustrated London News,* LXXXVIII (Saturday, June 26, 1886), front cover, 678–679. See also brief items on Ludwig II in "Parisian Sayings and Doings" and "The Court," *ILN,* LXXXVIII (Saturday, June 19, 1886), 645. See illustrations in *The Graphic,* XXXIII (Saturday, June 26, 1886), front cover, 684, 688. See also the following brief items pertaining to Ludwig II in the *Graphic:* under "Foreign," XXXIII (Saturday, June 12, 1886), 631; "King Ludwig," XXXIII (Saturday, June 19, 1886), 655; "The Royal Palace," XXXIV (Saturday, September 18, 1886), 307; and "Urn in which King Louis of Bavaria's Heart Lies," XXXIV (Saturday, September 18, 1886), 310.

[31] "King Louis of Bavaria," *The Spectator,* LIX (June 19, 1886), 806–807; "The Late King of Bavaria," and "Recent Bavarian Kings," *Saturday Review* (London), LXI (June 19, 1886), 834–835, 845–846; "Louis the Second of Bavaria," *Temple Bar,* LXXVII (August 1886), 511–528; H. Geffcken, "Contemporary Life and Thought in Germany," *The Contemporary Review,* L (August 1886), 277–280.

[32] "The Bavarian House of Wittelsbach," *Harper's Weekly Magazine,* XXX (Saturday, July 17, 1886), 459, 461; "Ludwig's Fitting End," *The Critic,* N.S. VI (July 3, 1886), 11.

Critic and the *Eclectic Magazine* reprinted the piece which had appeared in *Temple Bar*. "A Mad Monarch," by E. P. Evans, appeared in the *Atlantic Monthly* in October, and *Lippincott's Monthly Magazine* published "Ludwig of Bavaria: A Personal Reminiscence," by Lew Vanderpoole, in its November issue.[33] It is especially interesting to speculate that James may have seen the Vanderpoole article because its principal theme is Ludwig's admiration for Edgar Allan Poe and his attempts to explain his own temperament with reference to that of Poe. And James quotes "The Raven" in the exchange of repartee between Ford Obert and the narrator at the end of Chapter X of *The Sacred Fount:*

"Is the place wholly cleared of [the ladies]?"

"Save, it struck me [Obert], so far as they may have left some 'black plume as a token'——"

"Not, I trust," I returned, "of any 'lie' their 'soul hath spoken!' "[34]   (204)

But the *Atlantic* article is most notable among those pub-

[33] E. P. Evans, "A Mad Monarch," *The Atlantic Monthly,* LVIII (October 1886), 449–455; Lew Vanderpoole, "Ludwig of Bavaria: A Personal Reminiscence," *Lippincott's Monthly Magazine,* XXXVIII (November 1886), 535–539.

[34] James's reference is to the seventeenth stanza of "The Raven":
> "Be that word our sign of parting,
>   bird or fiend!" I shrieked, upstarting—
> "Get thee back into the tempest and the
>   Night's Plutonian shore!
> Leave no black plume as a token of that
>   lie thy soul hath spoken!
> Leave my loneliness unbroken!—quit the
>   bust above my door!
> Take thy beak from out my heart, and
>   take thy form from off my door!"
>   Quoth the Raven, "Nevermore."

lished in 1886 because it is the first one to attach the epithet of madness to Ludwig's name in its title, an epithet which was to become commonplace hereafter. It is also notable as one of the articles which James is most likely to have seen, for it faces the final page of the last installment of *The Princess Casamassima,* then being serialized in the *Atlantic.* Evans's theme, stated in the opening sentence, indicates the extent to which the king's story had become a case history in insanity by the autumn of 1886: "One of the most important and salutary lessons of modern science is that which teaches us to study history in the light of psycho-pathology." [35] Evans catalogues mad monarchs, comparing Ludwig with Domitian, Nero, George III, Frederick William I of Prussia, and "the German Emperor Rudolf II., who reigned and raged from 1576 to 1612." [36] He lists the king's serious injuries to his subjects under the influence of his madness: physical injuries, a murder, a presumptive manslaughter, confinement in a dungeon, banishments to America, the requirement that a man wear a black mask for a year, and so forth. He lists such "comparatively harmless hallucinations" of Ludwig's as paying homage to a certain tree, giving his benediction to a certain hedge, embracing a column at Linderhof after absences, and dining with the bust of Louis XIV.[37] Evans concludes with a portrait of Ludwig as "the central figure of much curious folklore" among the Bavarian peasantry: "In his castles, especially at Linderhof, he surrounded himself with scenes of the sagas and of fairyland; and as he dashed through the forests on winter nights, in a sleigh gorgeous with red and gold and blue and silver, and surmounted by two crowns glowing with electric light, no wonder the belated peasant turned aside with superstitious fear, and crossed

---

[35] Evans, "A Mad Monarch," p. 449.   [36] *Ibid.,* p. 454.
[37] *Ibid.,* p. 453.

himself, thinking the prince of mountain sprites was passing by." [38]

In 1887 a new theme begins to assert itself when the first
article appears in which the king's role as a builder rather
than his mental condition constitutes the central preoccupation.[39] Ludwig's palaces were opened to the general public
as a tourist attraction in August 1886,[40] and subsequent articles indicate a popular interest in them which was apparently encouraged by their nearness to the Oberammergau
Festival, held in 1890 and 1900: "Among the visitors to
Oberammergau this year many will make a point of visiting
the beautiful palaces which the late King Louis II. built
for himself in the Bavarian Highlands. Ten years ago these
places [palaces] were, of course, not open to the public; and
the most splendid of them all—that on the island of Herrenchiemsee—was still under scaffolding." [41] James himself went
to the Oberammergau Play in 1890 and must have heard talk
of the castles at this time whether or not he actually saw
them.[42] In October 1896 Linda Villari writes that "the late
King Ludwig's castles of Hohen Schwangau and Neu Schwanstein attract constant streams of travellers," [43] and by September 1898, even the interest of the peripatetic American tourist was being solicited by Alexander MacKay-Smith in *Harper's Monthly:* "The tourist in Bavaria who fails to see these

[38] *Ibid.,* p. 455.

[39] Bettina Wirth, "A Kingly Architect. Linderhof and Neu-
Schwanstein," *The Magazine of Art,* X (1887), 85–92.

[40] "Bavaria," London *Times,* July 31, 1886, p. 7.

[41] "The Palaces of an Artist King," London *Times,* June 7, 1890, p. 17.
Cf. Dora M. Jones, "The Royal Palaces of Bavaria and their Builders,"
Chambers's Journal, LXXVIII (Sixth Series, IV) (February 23, 1901),
199–201.

[42] *Letters,* ed. Lubbock, I, 166, 169.

[43] Linda Villari, "Linderhof," Supplement to *The Speaker,* XIV,
Saturday, October 3, 1896, 366.

creations of King Louis loses one of the most interesting trips in central Europe." [44]

Contemporary assessments of Ludwig's artistry reflect the same extremes of sentiment apparent in articles evaluating him as a ruler and assessing his relationship with Wagner. Especially at the beginning, critics rendered unqualified approval: "A life of incessant enjoyment of nature's charms, a life in which every day added some new beauty to the beauty amassed yesterday, a creative life to the last!" [45] "The palaces are much more magnificent than haphazard guesses described them to be, and they show that King Louis was gifted with a creative genius and with artistic taste for which he never obtained the right sort of credit during his lifetime." [46] Counter-charges are that the palaces satiate through a superfluity of amassed elegance and that they are imitative rather than original: "As for the interior of the little palace [of Linderhof], it combines the wildest luxury with the most execrable taste. . . . [In one room] one feels that the King must have aimed at expending the greatest possible amount of money on a very limited space. Such a jumble of precious things and jarring colours, of royal splendour and vulgar display!" [47] "As for those 'stately pleasure domes,' one may note that it is the magnificent site rather than the architecture of Neuschwanstein that is impressive, that Linderhof, modelled on the Petit Trianon, is a shrine erected to the memory of Marie Antoinette, and that Herrenschiemsee, a huge modern imitation of Versailles, is marred by its oppressive and taste-

[44] Alexander MacKay-Smith, "The Romance of a Mad King," *Harper's New Monthly Magazine,* XCVII (European edition, XXXVI) (September 1898), 596.

[45] Wirth, "A Kingly Architect," p. 85.

[46] "Palaces of an Artist King," p. 17.

[47] Villari, "Linderhof," p. 367.

less gorgeousness. The King, it will be seen, had no creative imagination." [48]

On the whole, Ludwig is more consistently represented as a patron of the arts and as a man frustrated in the development of his own artistic potential than as one whose personal achievement as an artist was notable. Either his obligations as ruler or the corrupting affliction of his madness is seen as having thwarted his development in the arts:

It is often difficult to draw a sharp line between oddness and lunacy, especially when eccentricity is relieved by a touch of genius, and it is quite conceivable that Louis II. might have attained eminence as a poet or a musician, if an uncongenial destiny had not weighted him with a crown.[49]

And it must be confessed that in these [the arts] he might, with proper application, have attained some personal distinction. The musical world owes him a debt of gratitude for his patronage of Wagner. He took a deep interest in painting and sculpture, and opened a lavish purse to encourage many other arts. But his chief claim to the remembrance of posterity will always be the palaces, or castles, which he built. Many of the most famous artists of Europe were occupied for years in designing and furnishing them.[50]

Frequently, Ludwig is represented as a man whose building activities were obsessive, as the victim of a craze, a compulsion, or a mania to build.[51] Or he is treated as a kind of

[48] "Ludwig II. of Bavaria" (anon. rev.), *Spectator,* LXXXIII (September 23, 1899), 415.

[49] "Recent Bavarian Kings," *Saturday Review* (London), LXI (June 19, 1886), 846. Cf. Leon Mead, "The Mad King," *Munsey's Magazine,* IX (August 1893), 526.

[50] MacKay-Smith, "The Romance of a Mad King," p. 596.

[51] E.g., MacKay-Smith, "The Romance of a Mad King," p. 605; Evans, "A Mad Monarch," p. 452.

transcendent child, a hero of romance, who built fairy palaces, gave substance to the Arabian Nights,[52] created a world of dreams which he preferred to that of everyday reality and into which he withdrew: "He showed an interested earnestness in trivial games and entertainments such as a child evinces in building card houses or in making mud pies—in short, pretending reality without seriously feeling it. Later on in the same manner he played at building palaces, at stage management with Wagner, at trying to give Bavaria a copy of Versailles, letting imagination rule all his actions."[53] A similar characterization is offered in a review article of Frances Gerard's biography in the London *Bookman* for October 1899. James is likely to have seen this latter article because photographs of him and several of his friends and acquaintances (Edmund Gosse, Paul Bourget, Emile Zola) appear in the same issue, in an extended review of *The Library of Famous Literature,* edited by Dr. Richard Garnett, to which they had contributed introductory essays.

The preoccupation with Ludwig as builder, artist, and patron of the arts was still current when *The Sacred Fount* appeared on February 15, 1901. One week later, on February 23, Dora M. Jones's article, "The Royal Palaces of Bavaria and Their Builders," a veritable treasury of Ludwigian clichés, appeared in *Chambers's Journal.* By the late 1890's, however, the Ludwig material was beginning to wear thin. This is indicated, for instance, in the remarks of two reviewers of Miss Gerard's book quoted above: "Still another version of the story of King Louis" and "an old and well-worn story." Writers begin to take shortcuts, assuming their readers' knowledge of the material: "The story of the life of King

[52] E.g., MacKay-Smith, "The Romance of a Mad King," p. 602.
[53] Leon Mead, "The Mad King," *Munsey's Magazine,* IX (August 1893), 527.

Louis II. of Bavaria is sufficiently familiar . . . to render any minute repetition of it needless." [54] Or: "It is needless to repeat the story that all the world knows of his association with Wagner." [55]

Undoubtedly one reason that Ludwig II remained of interest despite the lack of new material available is that he was inseparably a part of the Wagner biography. And the Wagner movement in England, firmly launched in the 1870's and hard fought in the 1880's, culminated triumphantly in the last decade of the century: "The eighteen-nineties are chiefly memorable in the history of British Wagnerism for the bringing to performance in the English language of most of the major music-dramas, and for the publication of a large amount of important literature on Wagner, both of these manifestations bearing witness to the fact that a large and interested Wagner public had now been created." [56] The degree to which Wagner had become fashionable in the nineties is suggested by an announcement in *The Meister,* quarterly publication of the British Wagner Society, on May 22, 1894: "We hear that the London booking for the Bayreuth Festival is larger than in any previous year, upwards of 5,000 seats having already been sold here." [57] In February 1898 the appearance of an English translation of H. S. Chamberlain's *Richard Wagner* led one reviewer to exclaim: "To judge by the enormous 'output' of books dealing directly with Wagnerian matters there must be an insatiable public somewhere. But do we not know now every single circumstance, internal and external, connected with the great man from his biretta to his slippers? Will there ever be an end to

[54] MacKay-Smith, "The Romance of a Mad King," p. 594.
[55] Jones, "The Royal Palaces of Bavaria," p. 200.
[56] Percy Scholes, *The Mirror of Music* (London, 1947), I, 255.
[57] "Notes," *The Meister*, VII, 64.

the making of books on this fruitful subject?" [58] Such books included, for example, the first English translation of Wagner's letters, making available his eulogies of the young king.

Another reason that Ludwig II remained newsworthy even to the end of the century is that two of his most distinguished cousins now died under extraordinary conditions and thereby set up a wave of biographical remembrance that carried him along in its wake. The first was Princess Sophie of Bavaria, Ludwig II's one-time fiancée. The reasons for their estrangement were never known, but several months after their betrothal the king terminated the engagement without explanation, and remained a bachelor for life. Princess Sophie later married into the House of Orléans and took a place at the head of Parisian society as the wife of the Duc d'Alençon and the niece by marriage of the Duc d'Aumale. James himself must have met her in Paris during the winter of 1876 at a reception given by the Duc d'Aumale.[59] On May 4, 1897, she was a patroness of an annual charity bazaar, which was in progress when one of the most terrible fires in French history occurred and she, together with scores of the Parisian élite, was burned to death. The story of this fire, that of the Duchess' personal heroism, and that of her burial all made a profound impression in England.[60] Then, on September 10, 1898, the Empress Elizabeth of Austria, an older sister of Princess Sophie and an intimate of Ludwig II till the end of his life, died under equally shocking conditions, stabbed to death by an assassin in Geneva. Her death was of

[58] *Literature* (anon. rev.), II (February 26, 1898), 229.

[59] See Leon Edel, *The Conquest of London: 1870–1881* (Philadelphia, 1962), p. 228: "Madame Laugel obtained for Henry an invitation to a ducal reception, where the American met members of the Orléans family, all save the Comte de Paris, pretender to the throne."

[60] See the London *Times* from May 5 through May 19, 1897; the *Illustrated London News* for May 8 and 15; the *Graphic* for May 15 and 22.

course a major news event throughout Europe, and like that of her sister, it gave rise to biographical reminiscences which included the late king.[61]

Finally, in September 1899, all these interrelated interests were once again nurtured by the appearance of the first English biography of the king. One reviewer noted that "Biographies of Royal personages, either living or dead, have enjoyed something of a vogue of late. We have had lives of the Empress Eugénie, and of the late Empress of Austria. Now we have, from Miss Frances Gerard, *The Romance of Ludwig II. of Bavaria*." [62] Whatever the complex of reasons, possibly because an awareness of the king had recently been aroused and refocused by events of international importance, Miss Gerard's book enjoyed a popular reception greater than one might have expected for a first book of no demonstrable literary merits by an unknown writer on a subject which was clearly becoming hackneyed. It was advertised by Hutchinson in the *Athenaeum* for the first time on September 23, 1899, and on October 14 a printing of a second thousand was announced for the following week.[63] It was reviewed in at least

[61] See the Bibliography at the end of this study for various items pertaining to the Empress Elizabeth which resuscitate Ludwig II.

[62] *Literature* (anon. rev.), V (December 23, 1899), 615. Frances A. Gerard is the pseudonym of Miss Geraldine Fitzgerald, an Irish-born gentlewoman who lived in London. She wrote some ten volumes, including popular biography and history on German and Irish themes, during the 1890's and early twentieth century. According to her Introduction, she became interested in Ludwig II while reading an article about him by A. De Burgh, "The Romance of a King," which had appeared in two installments in a women's magazine, *The Lady's Realm*, for March and April, 1898. This source of inspiration suggests the general level on which Frances Gerard works. The London *Times* reviewer described her book as one dealing with "an old and well-worn story" based on "materials . . . derived from no very recondite sources." ("Books of the Week" [anon. rev.], September 30, 1899, p. 12.)

[63] *The Athenaeum*, II (September 23, 1899), 405, and II (October 14, 1899), 509.

fifteen periodicals, including brief mention in *Punch*. And
several of these reviews, those in *The Spectator*, *The Academy*, and *The Bookman*, are substantial articles.[64] By 1901
it went into a second edition in both England and America.

Henry James was at work on *The Sacred Fount* during the
period when Frances Gerard's book appeared and was being
reviewed. His last entry in the *Notebooks* in anticipation of
using the "2 couples" *donnée* is dated May 16, 1899,[65] and
on August 9, 1900, he writes to William Dean Howells that
he has just completed the novel: "I have just finished, as it
happens, a fine flight (of eighty thousand words) *into* the high
fantastic, which has rather depleted me, or at any rate affected
me as discharging my obligations in that quarter." [66] It is
easy to see why the allusion to Ludwig might have occurred
to James at just this time in view of the pervasive contemporary interest: In the floodtide of Wagnerism, in the wake
of the Paris fire and the imperial assassination, and upon the
appearance of the first English biography, conversation
touching on the late king must have been everyday fare at
social gatherings during these years, and Ludwig II is a figure
of transcendent appeal to the imagination. Let us return,
then, to the question of just what connotations James was
presumably summoning up in making this allusion and their
consequent bearing upon the interpretation of *The Sacred
Fount*.

Collectively, contemporary articles treat the king, in somewhat perceptible waves of interest, as the eccentric monarch,

[64] Those review articles which I have seen are included in the Bibliography. In addition to these, Hutchinson & Co.'s advertisements quote
reviews of Miss Gerard's book which appeared in the *Daily Chronicle,*
the *Daily News,* the *Globe,* the *Liverpool Post,* the *Pall Mall Gazette,* the
Scotsman, and the *Standard.*

[65] *Notebooks,* p. 292.

[66] *Letters,* ed. Lubbock, I, 356–357.

the madman on the throne, and, finally, as the would-be-artist king. More specifically, the citation of ludicrous anecdotes and the charge of Wagnerism are commonplace means of demonstrating the king's eccentricity. Among the anecdotes those of his assuming the costumes of Lohengrin and of other Wagnerian heroes, indoor swan-boating and nocturnal sleigh rides, solitary midnight theatricals and various adventures with Marie Antoinette and Louis XIV are constantly reiterated. Wagner is commonly identified as an evil influence, variously responsible for Ludwig's neglect of his political duties, for his megalomania, for his tendency to withdraw into make-believe, for his building extravagances, and even for his failure to marry. In general, the king's treatment of Princess Sophie and his celibacy are more censured than praised. There are sometimes implications of sexual abnormality and of misogyny.

After Ludwig's deposition the imputation of madness is a fact which all writers must acknowledge, whether they choose to question the extremity of the diagnosis, to pity the king as a victim in whom hereditary disease blighted superior intellect and sensibility, or to insist upon his unfitness for rule. After the madness is no longer a matter for serious speculation, a new interest develops in Ludwig's palaces and, coincidentally, a new assessment of the king in the role of artist and builder. In general, he fares well as a patron of the arts, especially toward the end of the century, when a higher assessment is put upon Wagner's music. But his personal achievement as an artist is frequently qualified, either his uncongenial political duties or his madness being cited as cause for his failure to realize his artistic potential. He is frequently treated as a figure out of high romance or out of folklore who gave substance to a world of dreams and realized in everyday life things which ordinary men can only imagine.

Hence to his more sympathetic critics he transcended everyday life, and to the more severe he escaped from it by means of the satisfaction of his personal compulsions to build the palaces and to live as he wished. This complex of attitudes is epitomized in Miss Gerard's book, which appears to be virtually a compendium of contemporary opinion gleaned from periodical and other popular literature. One of her critics writes: "Louis came to his end thirteen years ago. Already he is a legend to the peasants of Bavaria, and only when he has become so to the rest of the world, when the laugh at his eccentricities, and the irritation at his play-acting have died down, will the essentials of him be rightly known. Miss Gerard now apologises, now seems to stretch her charity even to the point of approval, but she leaves the impression that as a sensible person with a sense of duty and responsibility, she has an unbounded contempt for him." [67]

It is apparent that attitudes about the king had not crystallized into any one clear image at the time when James was writing. Ludwig exists, certainly, as a figure of the artist in contemporary accounts, but this figure is constantly qualified, first by the broadcast anecdotes about his ludicrous behavior, then by the omnipresent fact of his madness, and finally, by diversified opinion over whether the palaces are truly works of art magnificently conceived or monuments to costly vulgarity and personal whim. The portrait of the artist coexists with that of the inadequate ruler, the megalomaniac ruler, the patron of the arts, the romantic fairy-tale hero, the crackpot with humorous implications, even that of the misogynist or the sexual aberrant. Hence it is unlikely that James would have made this allusion if he had wished the narrator to be taken seriously as a type of the artist, or his theory to

[67] "Wagner's Fairy Prince" (anon. rev.), *Bookman,* XVII (October 1899), 27.

stand as a work of art, because at best Ludwig is an ambiguous figure and at worst he is a ridiculous one. Furthermore, James's reference is to Ludwig's midnight operas, and this association would have recalled the king's humorous idiosyncrasies to a contemporary audience. The particular allusion James has made invites an amused response and therefore supports further the general thesis presented in this essay, that James's emphasis was on the joke rather than its implications. I can only wonder how James Reaney would reconcile this interpretation of the allusion with his election of a phrase in the same sentence with Ludwig II (quoted at the beginning of this chapter) as the theme of the novel. In "attempting to prove that James's theme is here the triumph of art, of light over dark," [68] he judges that "the theme of the work is contained in a phrase from it: 'the condition of light.' " [69]

Most important, however, the concept of madness as it pertains to Ludwig II is clearly pathological. And I stress this point because the most recent, and to my sense the most cogent of all interpretations of *The Sacred Fount* as a parable of the artist's creative experience, invites us to understand Mrs. Brissenden's final imputation of madness to the narrator in a figurative rather than a literal sense. The following exchange occurs less than twenty pages before the "Ludwig" passage:

"Well," said Mrs. Briss, "I think you're crazy."
It naturally struck me. "Crazy?"
"Crazy."
I turned it over. "But do you call that intelligible?"
She did it justice. "No: I don't suppose it *can* be so for you if you *are* insane."

[68] "The Condition of Light," p. 148.   [69] *Ibid.,* p. 140.

I risked the long laugh which might have seemed that of madness. " 'If I am' is lovely!" And whether or not it was the special sound, in my ear, of my hilarity, I remember just wondering if perhaps I mightn't be. "Dear woman, it's the point at issue!"

But it was as if she too had been affected. "It's not at issue for me now."   (278)

The narrator himself has also bantered with this conception at an earlier stage of his inquiry: "Is not this small touch perhaps the best example I can give of the intensity of amusement I had at last enabled my private madness to yield me?" (162)

Tony Tanner, in "Henry James's Subjective Adventurer," defines madness in *The Sacred Fount* as "the verdict of the practical world, the people who make themselves at home amongst the surface facts." [70] He identifies madness with misapprehension; it is the false estimate rendered by the undiscerning who fail to perceive essences, among whom he mistakenly reckons Mrs. Brissenden:

The narrator of *The Sacred Fount* is at least eligible for Shaftesbury's definition of the artist as 'a second maker; a just Prometheus under Jove.' It is James's peculiarly modern insight—think of Mann's *Doctor Faustus*—to allow the suggestion that the activities of the artist might be allied to insanity. But then, who should have the last word on health in a disease-damaged world? Perhaps here we should recall the moving dying words of the artist Dencombe in *The Middle Years:* there can be little doubt that he speaks for James. 'We work in the dark—we do what we can—we give what we have. Our doubt is our passion and our passion is our task. The rest is the madness of art.' [71]

[70] "Henry James's Subjective Adventurer," p. 47.   [71] *Ibid.,* p. 55.

Landon C. Burns, Jr., takes a harder view of the narrator, yet allows for the idea of his "craziness" in a similar way; that is, this imputation is a kind of symbolic reckoning visited upon an unworthy "artist" figure who overreaches himself:

The artist must not either betray his role of providence in the realm of art lest he destroy the unconsciousness of his subjects, nor may he attempt to alter what he sees except when he transfers his observations to his art. . . . If the artist falls into either of these traps (and there is a clear indication that the narrator here may have fallen into both), then not only has he exceeded what is permitted him as observer in the real world, but he has also destroyed himself as artist. Though the world of art has a separate existence, it draws that life from the real world; at the same time, if the artist-observer overreaches himself, then he must be driven out, called "crazy," and this is tantamount to his destruction in the world of art.[72]

Ludwig II, however, is not the professional, the master artist, such as the fictional Dencombe. He gives rise not only to the ideas of patronage, of dilettantism, of unrealized potentiality, but inescapably, to that of disease. James would certainly have been obscuring his theme by associating the narrator with such a figure, whether he were writing a story either about a consummate artist or about one who failed through excess to exercise his function legitimately. The associations which the allusion evokes are more congenial with the estimates of those critics who have seen in the narrator "a case of incipient lunacy" [73] or of "pathological obsession." [74] The presence of Ford Obert in *The Sacred Fount,* a profes-

[72] Henry James's Mysterious Fount," pp. 524–525.
[73] Robert Marks, *James's Later Novels* (New York, 1960), p. 13.
[74] J. A. Ward, "The Ineffectual Heroes," p. 326.

sional artist specifically identified as such, also implies that the narrator is not necessarily an artist to the extent that he believes himself to be. A significant point of contrast between them is that Obert characteristically prefers the simpler explanation to the more complex. Furthermore, though Obert strives to understand, he admits it when he does not. And finally, James inserts midway in the narrator's own account a qualification of his artistry: "To see all this was at the time, I remember, to be as inhumanly amused as if one had found one could create something. I had created nothing but a clue or two to the larger comprehension I still needed, yet I positively found myself overtaken by a mild artistic glow" (104).

The association with Ludwig II may, on the other hand, encourage us to see the narrator as a type of the *artiste manqué* who, as Quentin Anderson has described him, "plays at being an artist in life, and for this reason denies life its rights." [75] In this character he also resembles Mrs. Gereth in *The Spoils of Poynton* (1897), another book of James's transitional middle period, because his relationship to his theory is analogous to Mrs. Gereth's relationship to her collection of art objects. Both characters are artists of a kind because each has created an external symbol of himself, which is an object of devotion. Both do so at the expense of certain human values: Mrs. Gereth is willing to sacrifice the moral sensibility of her friend Fleda Vetch to the cause of preserving the art treasures which she has assembled, while the narrator loses both his decorum and his human sympathy for the supposed victims in his passion to perfect and sustain his intellectual artifact. That the narrator should ultimately come to believe absolutely in his own theory, then, suggests that he, like Mrs. Gereth, is laboring under a compulsive impulse at self-

[75] *The American Henry James,* p. 222, n. 17.

preservation when his position is challenged by another character. It also implies that James perhaps became more interested in his character's obsessive struggle for identity or for self-realization than in the intrinsic product of his fancy. Possibly this was also the nature of his interest in Ludwig II. Could James have seen Miss Gerard's book? The king had written: "The building of my castles *must* proceed, and that will give me new life." The narrator, under fire from Mrs. Brissenden, remarks, " 'It's simply that my theory is dead and that the blight of the rest is involved' " (288).[76]

Aside from throwing light on James's supposed intention in writing *The Sacred Fount,* and raising very real questions about the plausibility of the "artist" theory, the Ludwig passage also calls attention to another very interesting issue, the implications of which I can only hint at here. And that is the question of how much light may yet be thrown on James's fiction, and perhaps upon his general interests and preoccupations, by a more thoroughgoing inquiry into his allusive language than has so far been attempted. Increasingly, critics have observed that a very substantial part is played in both the fiction and the critical writing by literary and other allusions. Alexander Holder-Barrell made a gesture in this direction by pointing out the prevalence of allusions to Thackeray, Shakespeare, Dickens, George Eliot, Goethe, and others, but he is interested in them principally as a type of "obscuring" image, and speaks only in general terms.[77] William T. Stafford has attempted to form some estimate of the

[76] For another, to me convincing, argument in support of the conclusion that we have here a type of the *artiste manqué,* see Ralph A. Ranald, "James's Portrait of the Artist *Manqué,* especially pp. 244–245, 247.

[77] *The Development of Imagery and Its Functional Significance in Henry James's Novels,* The Cooper Monographs on English and American Language and Literature, ed. H. Lüdeke (Bern, 1959), p. 30.

part allusions play in the Prefaces.[78] And most recently Robert L. Gale has included what amounts to annotated checklists of allusions arranged according to topics in his study of Jamesian imagery. But no substantial interpretative work has yet been done on allusions in their proper contexts and in cross references. The reference to Ludwig II, for instance, not only appears to have significant bearing on the interpretation of the novel, but also calls our attention to the fact that James was susceptible to the tremendous current preoccupation with the Wagner movement and reflected it in the texture of his fiction.

Many English novelists included Wagner as part of the local color of the times: Mrs. Humphry Ward in *Robert Elsmere* (1888), for example, Oscar Wilde in *The Picture of Dorian Gray* (1891), Robert Hichens in *The Green Carnation* (1894). George Du Maurier's *Trilby* (1894) satirizes Wagner in the character of Svengali. A performance of *Tannhäuser* in E. E. Benson's *The Rubicon* (1894) forewarns the hero of the seductive charms of a certain young matron. And George Moore's hero in *Mike Fletcher* (1889) seeks confirmation for his *Weltschmerz* in Wagner, while his heroine in *Evelyn Innes* (1898) and *Sister Teresa* (1901) is a Wagnerian singer.[79] Likewise, in James's fiction the allusion to Ludwig II is one in a sequence of at least eight references to aspects of the Wagner material.

In 1883, the year of Wagner's death, James has the narrator of "The Impressions of a Cousin" remark: "This young man

[78] "Literary Allusions in James's Prefaces," *American Literature,* XXXV (March 1963), 60–70.

[79] For these and other examples of the influence of Wagnerism on contemporary English literature, see Max Moser, *Richard Wagner in der englischen Literatur des XIX. Jahrhunderts,* Schweizer Anglistische Arbeiten, No. 7 (Bern, 1938), pp. 55–56, 78–79, 81, 91, 94, and Scholes, *Mirror of Music,* I, 256.

asked me ever so many questions about my cousin. . . . Some
of his questions were certainly idle. What can it matter to him
whether she has one little dog or three, or whether she is an
admirer of the music of the future?" [80] In 1892 James surprisingly introduces a German, "a born Bavarian," as his
hero in "Collaboration," a story which embodies the idea
that art embraces a community of men in a more profound
and significant way than national patriotism may do. This
idea is illustrated through the collaboration of the Bavarian
composer and a French poet, who are brought into harmony
of feeling by Wagner's music: " '*Foilà—foilà!*' cried the
musician, and with hands for an instant suspended he wan-
dered off into mysterious worlds. He played Wagner, and
then Wagner again—a great deal of Wagner; in the midst of
which, abruptly, he addressed himself again to Vendemer,
who had gone still farther from the piano, launching to me,
however, from his corner a '*Dieu, que c'est beau!*' which I
saw that Heidenmauer caught. 'I've a conception for an
opera, you know—I'd give anything if you'd do the
libretto!' " [81] Here James is apparently drawing on his own
experience in having listened to endless recitals of Wagner,
for Mr. Edel describes him as having passed many similar
evenings with less exalted feelings than those depicted in the
story: "Late in the year [1876] at Paul Zhukovsky's he listens
from 9 to 2 A.M. to a young pianist playing selections from

[80] In *Tales of Three Cities* (Boston, 1884), p. 20. This story was first
published in the *Century Magazine, XXVII* (November–December 1883),
116–129, 257–275. See p. 120.

[81] In *The Wheel of Time* (New York, 1893), pp. 102, 127–128. This
story was first published in the *English Illustrated Magazine, IX* (September 1892), 911–921, where the phrase "a born Bavarian" originally
read "a Saxon by birth" (p. 912). The second passage (on p. 917) is identical with the one quoted above except for minor variations in spelling
and punctuation.

Wagner's operas, then in their early French vogue, before a small Russian circle. 'I enjoyed the circle, but I had an over-dose of Wagner, whom Zhukovsky vastly admires.' " [82] In 1896 the narrator of "Glasses" hurries to the opera upon his return from abroad: "Within a week after my return to London I went to the opera, of which I had always been much of a devotee. I arrived too late for the first act of 'Lohengrin,' but the second was just beginning, and I gave myself up to it with no more than a glance at the house." And his judgment reflects the pervasive enthusiasm of the times: "The music was supreme, Wagner passed first." [83] In 1899 the socially conscious but impecunious Mrs. Brooken-ham considers "allowing" Mitchy to take her and her husband to Bayreuth in *The Awkward Age*.[84] This would of course have been the fashionable place to go, and the allusion is a significant detail in Mrs. Brookenham's predatory social odyssey.

Oscar Cargill finds in *Tristan und Isolde* a "precipitant" and "catalyzer" for *The Wings of the Dove* (1902), which is James's next fiction (after *The Sacred Fount* in 1901) to in-clude a Wagnerian allusion: "In an arresting figure Henry James compares the trip of Milly Theale and Mrs. Stringham up through Italy and across the Alps, before the heroine's tragedy begins, to a Wagnerian overture. What follows then, in *The Wings of the Dove,* is a Wagnerian opera, another

[82] Edel, *The Conquest of London,* p. 229; cf. p. 405: James's overdose was apparently still in effect in 1880 when he passed up a chance to meet the " 'musician of the future.' "

[83] In *Embarrassments* (New York, 1896), pp. 166–167, 174. This story was first published in the *Atlantic Monthly,* LXXVII (February 1896), 145–173, where both the passages quoted here also appear (on pp. 169, 171) with minor variations.

[84] *The Awkward Age* (New York and London, 1899), p. 236.

composition on the *Liebestod* theme." [85] Mr. Cargill goes on
to speculate that other versions of the Tristan legend may
have been helpful to James in formulating his own treatment
of the theme. This is the very sort of speculative insight into
imaginative origins and influences to which I believe seemingly casual allusions in James's fiction may consistently give
rise.[86] Finally, Robert Gale has noted at least two other
Wagnerian allusions in the late fiction, in *The Golden Bowl*
(1904) and *The Ivory Tower* (posthumous), respectively:
"Maggie, once she is realistically married to her Prince,
'ceased to see . . . the pair of operatic, of high Wagnerian
lovers . . . interlocked in their wood of enchantment.' . . .
And loud, large Rosanna Gaw of *The Ivory Tower* 'ring[s]
out like Brünnhilde at the opera.'" Basing his statement
upon these two instances together with the passages from *The
Sacred Fount* and *The Wings of the Dove*, Mr. Gale concludes, "Regularly, then, Wagner is called upon when James
wishes to suggest the unrealistic, the romantic, or the gro-
tesque." [87] This statement is only half true, I believe, judging
by other passages which I have catalogued above. But here I
want simply to re-emphasize the point that these seemingly
incidental passages, taken either separately or in association
with others which evoke similar associations, may be a source
of very considerable insight to the more conscientious student
of James or to persons interested in imaginative origins and
influences upon works of fiction.

We see in the present instance that the allusion to Ludwig

[85] *Novels of Henry James*, pp. 338–339.

[86] For other illustrations of such relationships, see Jean H. Frantz,
"Henry James and Saintine," *Notes and Queries*, VII (July 1960), 266–
268, pp. 160–161 below and Robert E. Spiller's résumé of such studies in
Eight American Authors (New York, 1963), pp. 401–402.

[87] *The Caught Image*, pp. 137–138.

II is only one in a sequence of passages which indicate James's constant awareness of the Wagnerian atmosphere that hung over London in these years. And its presence therefore calls into question such an estimate of James's outlook in the late nineties as this one by Mr. Wilson: "It has for the time become difficult for James to sustain his old objectivity: he has relapsed into a dreamy interior world, where values are often uncertain and where it is not even possible any longer for him to judge his effect on his audience." [88] Far from being withdrawn into his own problems and disappointments during the postdramatic years, James, in these instances at least, demonstrates a characteristic awareness of contemporary preoccupations. And he must certainly have expected the readers of his day to recognize the allusive passage in *The Sacred Fount* as a meaningful clue. Or, our particular preoccupation with Ludwig II may lead us to observe that all three of these allusions in *The Sacred Fount* (like that to Cinderella noted on page 138, below) perform a common function of ironic commentary. If Ludwig is an unhappy bedfellow for the narrator, may the citation of "The Raven" (see page 101, above) be equally ominous for Mrs. Brissenden? What can be the significance of Obert's reference to (feminine) duplicity occurring as it does just before her final appearance and her absolute assertion that everything is "all right," if not to suggest that someone is lying? This appears to be one of the subtler means by which James points up Mrs. Brissenden's personal stake in the last interview and the length to which she will go to defend herself. Likewise, the narrator's identification of the lady of his quest with the nymph Egeria ironically intimates May Server's real plight in relation to him: "Ovid has told how Egeria, disconsolate when Numa died, melted into tears and became a fountain

[88] Wilson, "Ambiguity of Henry James," p. 134.

herself." [89] Finally, it is even tempting to speculate that, rather than being merely a passing allusion thrown in by James to guide his reader, the idea of Ludwig II may also have been an imaginative source for him in the formation of the novel. But this is a question to which I should like to return in Chapter 6, after the whole of my interpretation of the novel is before the reader.[90]

[89] See Mr. Edel's discussion of the reference to Egeria in his "Introductory Essay" to the Grove Press reprint of *The Sacred Fount,* from which I quote here, p. xxvii.

[90] Since I completed this consideration of allusions in *The Sacred Fount,* Professor Marjorie Kaufman of the Department of English at Mount Holyoke College has called my attention to another interesting verbal echo. James's narrator speaks of "the power not one's self, in the given instance, that made for passion" (17). Surely this passage has a literary antecedent in the opening paragraph of chapter II of Matthew Arnold's *Literature and Dogma,* where Arnold characterizes one religious first principle in these terms: "There is an enduring power, not ourselves, which makes for righteousness." James also quotes Arnold in *The Awkward Age.* Mrs. Brook, musing on what the Brookenhams may expect from Mr. Longdon, "saw it steadily and saw it whole," just as Sophocles contemplated life in "Dover Beach."

CHAPTER 5

Symbolic Implications
of the Narrator's Adventure

THOUGH James may have wished initially to perplex his reader, I do not believe that he ever expected the discriminating reader to be wholly unable to grasp the objective truths of the novel. There are too many incongruities in its texture that consistently work against the narrator by implication. And if one can perceive the grounds for doubting the narrator, it is no more difficult to construct an alternative set of hypotheses to account for appearances. Lady John, Brissenden, Obert, and Mrs. Briss all perceive and enunciate aspects of the truth, and the reader must simply reorient his point of view, turning to them, and to the figurative language of the novel, for direction. Nonetheless, there are clearly more serious undertones in *The Sacred Fount* than an interpretation of the novel merely as a *jeu d'esprit* or as high comedy would adequately explain. The central metaphor of the sacred fount is sinister, the central portrait in the Newmarch gallery, fatal, in its implications. In this chapter, therefore, I will inquire into these subtler, or symbolic, implications of the book, which seem to me most clearly to constitute a statement upon the relationship of the capacity to love and the power to live life fully.

One knows from the *Notebooks* that James's idea for the

novel originated in two related equations: "The notion of the young man who marries an older woman and who has the effect on her of making her younger and still younger, while he himself becomes her age. When he reaches the age that *she* was (on their marriage), she has gone back to the age that *he* was.—Mightn't this be altered (perhaps) to the idea of cleverness and stupidity? . . . The two things—the two elements—beauty and 'mind,' might be correspondingly, concomitantly exhibited as in the history of two related couples—with the opposition, in each case, that would help the thing to be dramatic." [1] These equations of course have psychological implications for the biographer, and both Leon Edel and Maxwell Geismar have discussed the book in relation to James's own attitudes: "The idea of depletion is a common one among many men who think of sex as a depleting force. Henry James seems to have held some such view." [2] But the fact that James originally thought of his *donnée* as suitable only for a short story [3] suggests that he himself initially saw his subject in external, perhaps even in graphic, terms rather than in philosophic or psychological ones. How might he objectify these equations in terms of character? Once under way, however, James seems to have been visited with his usual impulse to achieve depth as well as ironic effect, and perhaps for this reason gradually developed the symbolic implications of his material. Or he may simply have needed more substance with which to work in order to sustain his joke: the reader would find out the narrator much more quickly than he does if it were not for James's habit of con-

[1] *Notebooks,* pp. 150–151.
[2] Leon Edel, "An Introductory Essay," p. xxv. See also Mr. Edel's *The Untried Years* (Philadelphia, 1953), pp. 53–55, and Mr. Geismar's whole chapter on *The Sacred Fount* in *Henry James and the Jacobites.*
[3] *Letters,* ed. Lubbock, I, 408.

stantly taking up a subject and dropping it, treating various subjects in alternation so that points relevant to each other do not fall in too close sequence.[4] For whatever reason, then, the symbolic comment is "submerged" to an uncommon degree even for a James novel so that the reader must, with some trepidation, construct it almost entirely from the figurative and descriptive imagery of the book considered in relation to the ideas symbolized in the sacred fount and in the enigmatic portrait in Chapter IV.

The narrator's wording as he muses over whether Mrs. Brissenden would age suddenly if Briss were to die, suggests that he may have been thinking, simply, of the fountain of youth in adopting the metaphor of the sacred fount: "She would have loved his youth, and have made it her own, in death [i.e., his death] as in life, and he would have quitted the world, in truth, only the more effectually to leave it to her" (100).[5] The more notable fact is not, I believe, what the fount

---

[4] This practice is the constructional reason, I believe, for the disproportion between the length and the substance of the novel. The symbolic theme tends to receive its primary impetus in the even chapters; the social, in the odd. The weakest chapters in the book, by far, are IX through XI, in which James is trying to bridge the gap between the absolute assurance of the narrator in VIII, the first climax of the novel, and his absolute downfall in XII through XIV. The final chapters, though XIII especially is overtreated, are by no means anticlimactic, because they provide the assurances for which the reader has been waiting.

[5] For other possibilities see Andreas, "the power which enables a person to retain his bearings in life and to see life with an accurate and disinterested eye" (*Henry James and the Expanding Horizon*, p. 91); Blackmur, "conscience" ("The Sacred Fount," pp. 351–352); Ozick, "self-realization, the completion of the potentialities of the self" ("The Jamesian Parable," p. 69); Tintner, "the springs . . . of human behavior" ("The Spoils of Henry James," p. 248); and Parker Tyler, "that baptismal source that converts 'the actuality pretentious and vain' into 'the case rich and edifying' " ("*The Sacred Fount:* 'The Actuality Pretentious and Vain' vs. 'The Case Rich and Edifying," *Modern Fiction Studies,* IX [Summer 1963], 138). F. O. Matthiessen (*Henry James: The Major*

symbolizes—call it life or vitality or youth—but its situation in another person. To speak of the fount as a source of physical or of intellectual vitality for Mrs. Brissenden and Gilbert Long, therefore, is by implication to speak of a source of physical and intellectual depletion for Briss and the unknown lady. To quaff the vitality of another is, by inversion, to anticipate his age, or, ultimately, his death. And for the narrator to inquire into the origin of life in one pair is for him simultaneously to inquire into the origin of death in the other. He makes this point incidentally when he first presents the concept of the sacred fount, but in so flippant a metaphor that the idea of death is de-emphasized: " 'But the sacred fount is like the greedy man's description of the turkey as an "awkward" dinner dish. It may be sometimes too much for a single share, but it's not enough to go round' " (29). He also partially misleads the reader by pronouncing that the "larger mystery" toward the understanding of which he gropes is one such as preoccupies "minds for which the vision of life is an obsession" (23). In actuality he is not preoccupying himself more with life than with death in inquiring into the relationships of the Brissendens, of Long and the unknown lady, and his findings on the latter subject both constitute the symbolic statement of the novel and create another level of irony as the narrator, apparently unwittingly at the time, acts out his part in a symbolic drama.

If the idea of death is implicit in the metaphor of the

Phase [New York, 1944], p. 72) and Edmund Wilson ("Ambiguity of Henry James," pp. 125–126) have both speculated that James had sexual vitality or love in mind. Quentin Anderson traces James's title to the books of *Zechariah* and *Ecclesiastes* and the fountain of life (*American Henry James,* pp. 223–224), and Ralph A. Ranald also thinks that it is "the fountain of life" ("The Sacred Fount," p. 240). James K. Folsom discusses the fount with reference to both *Ecclesiastes* and Archimago's well ("Archimago's Well: An Interpretation of *The Sacred Fount*," *Modern Fiction Studies,* VII (Summer 1961), 143–144.

sacred fount, it is more forcefully represented in the mysterious portrait in the Newmarch gallery.[6] Just as the conversation with Mrs. Brissenden in Chapter III is a kind of pass key to the true state of affairs on the social level of the novel, so the interpretation of the portrait in Chapter IV is a kind of pass key to the symbolic statement. This painting, the narrator comments, is " 'the picture, of all pictures, that most needs an interpreter' " (55). If the reader were to pause here, before considering the conflicting opinions of the characters, might it occur to him, tentatively, that the picture of all pictures that most needs an interpreter is death? The subsequent description of the figure bears out this inference: "a young man in black—a quaint, tight black dress, fashioned in years long past; with a pale, lean, livid face and a stare, from eyes without eyebrows, like that of some whitened old-world clown" (55). Like the figure, death is young and yet of remote origin; pale or livid of hue; sometimes lean, sometimes with staring eyes. What of the mask the figure holds— "a representation of a human face, modelled and coloured,

[6] Cf. brief comments on the portrait in Allott, "Henry James and the Fantasticated Conceit: *The Sacred Fount*," *The Northern Miscellany*, No. 1 (Autumn 1953), pp. 81–83, and "Symbol and Image in the Later Work of Henry James," *Essays in Criticism*, III (July 1953), 328–329; Andreach, "Henry James's *The Sacred Fount*," p. 200; Bowden, *Themes of Henry James*, p. 87; Burns, "Henry James's Mysterious Fount," pp. 525–526; Finkelstein, "The 'Mystery' of Henry James's *The Sacred Fount*," pp. 758–759; Folsom, "Archimago's Well," pp. 139–140; Arnold P. Hinchliffe, "Henry James's *The Sacred Fount*," *Texas Studies in Literature and Language*, II (Spring 1960), 93; Krook, *Ordeal of Consciousness*, p. 177, n. 1; Reaney, "The Condition of Light," pp. 143–144; Stevenson, *Crooked Corridor*, pp. 97–98; Tintner, "Spoils of Henry James," pp. 247–248; Walter F. Wright, *The Madness of Art* (Lincoln, Nebr., 1962), pp. 187–188. Leon Edel has discussed it more fully in "An Introductory Essay," pp. xvi–xx; Oscar Cargill, in *The Novels of Henry James*, pp. 290–292; and Robert L. Gale, in *"The Marble Faun* and *The Sacred Fount:* A Resemblance," *Studi Americani*, VIII (Rome, 1962), 21–33.

in wax, in enamelled metal, in some substance not human"? (55) Its most notable characteristics are that it resembles a human face and yet is not human: might this also be a description of death? At this point Mrs. Server proposes that the painting could be called " 'the Mask of Death' " (56), a paradoxical name because it may be understood to mean either the mask that represents or signifies Death, or the mask that belongs to Death. Suppose both meanings applied. Then might the portrait symbolize death in two of its aspects? For death may appear either masked or unmasked in different men.

The characters begin to discuss the painting, and the narrator argues that the mask is Life because, like Life, it is " 'blooming and beautiful.' " " 'It's the man's own face that's Death' " (56). Ignoring Mrs. Server's dissension, he goes on, then, to speculate whether the man in the painting is putting on or taking off the mask. Is he, in other words, represented as being in a moment of taking up life or of casting it off? Since the reader by Chapter IV has ample reason to question the narrator's interpretations, however, let him compare May Server's interpretation of the painting, especially in view of the fact that for all her gentleness of manner she does not back down in the face of the narrator's disagreement. In interpreting her remarks the reader ought, further, to bear in mind an observation that the narrator has made earlier in this same chapter about Mrs. Server's conversation: "I give rather the sense than the form [of her remarks], for they were a little scattered and troubled, and I helped them out and pieced them together" (49). Perhaps one must piece together what she says about the portrait in order to arrive at her sense:

"Yes, what in the world does it mean?" Mrs. Server replied. "One could call it—though that doesn't get one much further—the Mask of Death."

"Why so?" I demanded while we all again looked at the picture. "Isn't it much rather the Mask of Life? It's the man's own face that's Death. The other one, blooming and beautiful——"

"Ah, but with an awful grimace!" Mrs. Server broke in.

"The other one, blooming and beautiful," I repeated, "is Life, and he's going to put it on; unless indeed he has just taken it off."

"He's dreadful, he's awful—that's what I mean," said Mrs. Server. "But what does Mr. Long think?"

"The artificial face, on the other hand," I went on, as Long now said nothing, "is extremely studied and, when you carefully look at it, charmingly pretty. I don't see the grimace."

"I don't see anything else!" Mrs. Server good-humouredly insisted.   (55–6)

The mask, then, is not life to Mrs. Server because to her it has a tell-tale grimace, which the narrator does not see. Interrupted, she restates her point, that what she means (by saying that the mask has an awful grimace) is that the *man* in the painting is "dreadful," is "awful." Hence she is equating the awfulness of the mask with that of the man. Her remarks, like her name for the portrait, imply that, paradoxically, the mask and the man are one.

Now the discussion of the painting concludes with Long, Obert, Mrs. Server, and the narrator agreeing that the man in the portrait resembles Brissenden, while Obert and the narrator agree that the " 'grinning mask' " (56) resembles Mrs. Server. If one now discards the narrator's interpretation of the painting, that it represents life and death in some sort of indefinite relationship, for Mrs. Server's implied interpretation, that it is death in two aspects, one then emerges with this tentative identification: Brissenden and May are simply the emblems of two kinds of death; the death, one might say, tentatively, of the body, which manifests itself in outward signs, and of the mind or spirit, which may conceal itself to some extent beneath a blooming and beautiful exterior. Working with this concept, the reader will find that he has a key to the symbolic implications of *The Sacred Fount*.[7]

Brissenden comes closer to functioning as an emblematic character than any other in the novel. He is consistently portrayed as being in a state of physical decline: "Fatigued, fixed, settled, he seemed to have piled up the years. . . . It was as if he had discovered some miraculous short cut to the common doom" (22). He is " 'as fine, as swaddled, as royal a mummy, to the eye, as one would wish to see' " (27). If Mrs. Brissenden's state has become " 'bloated,' " Guy's is now a " 'shrunken one' " (67), his identity, " 'blighted' " (151). Silence attaches to his presence: Mrs. Server may sit together with him " 'without sound' " (172). But so, even, may the garrulous Lady John (101): "What Lady John's famous intellect seemed to draw most from Brissenden's presence was the liberty to rest" (101–2). The idea of dryness attaches to his manner (107). "There was as little of the common in his dry, distinguished patience as in the case I had made out for him. Blighted and ensconed [sic], he looked at it over the rigid convention, his peculiar perfection of necktie, shirt-front and waistcoat, as some aged remnant of sovereignty at

[7] The fact that these characters have a symbolic identity, and the narrator himself a symbolic role to play, is one reason for the reader's difficulty in interpreting the novel. There appears to be no consistent means, except trial and error, by which the reader can gauge when he is to understand a certain passage with reference to developments in the social foreground of the novel or with reference to the drama symbolically enacted in the background or both. Since he is meanwhile trying to distinguish an objective "truth" from the views of that truth presented by the narrator and each of his various interlocutors, to have also to distinguish a symbolic statement (a confidence between himself and the author) requires that the reader simultaneously differentiate four different patterns of development. To do so is virtually impossible except retrospectively.

the opera looks over the ribbon of an order and the ledge of
a box" (158). Briss's fount is running dry simply because it is
constantly diverted to satisfy Mrs. Brissenden's demands upon
him: "The same poor Briss as before his brief adventure
[with Mrs. Server], he was only feeling afresh in his soul, as
a response to [his wife], the gush of the sacred fount" (198).
Meanwhile Mrs. Brissenden's own stream of life widens into
a flood: "What was actually before me was the positive pride
of life and expansion, the amplitude of conscious action and
design; not the arid channel forsaken by the stream, but the
full-fed river sweeping to the sea, the volume of water, the
stately current, the flooded banks into which the source had
swelled" (245). By the end of the second day, having func-
tioned primarily as a symbolic figure of death rather than as
a character in the social situation, Brissenden enacts a symbolic decease. Bringing his wife's message to the narrator
after midnight, it seems, is Brissenden's final sacrifice to his
wife's demands: "This circumstance seemed to have placed
him again at the very bottom of his hole. It was down in that
depth that he let [the narrator] see him—it was out of it that
he delivered himself" (225). Then, while the narrator stands
by helpless—"*I* stood for the hollow chatter of the vulgar
world" (226)—Brissenden finally withdraws:

He looked round the room—at the two or three clusters of men
. . . he looked over an instant at Ford Obert, whose eyes, I thought,
he momentarily held. It was absolutely as if, for me, he were seeking such things—out of what was closing over him—for the last
time. Then he turned again to the door, which, just not to fail
humanly to accompany him a step, I had opened. On the other
side of it I took leave of him. The passage, though there was a
light in the distance, was darker than the smoking-room, and I
had drawn the door to.

. . . With a short, sharp "Good-bye!" he completely released himself. . . .

Ford Obert has since told me that when I came back to him there were tears in my eyes, and I didn't know at the moment how much the words with which he met me took for granted my consciousness of them. "He looks a hundred years old!" (226–8)

The same kind of symbolic identity attaches to Mrs. Server, but it is somewhat more complexly represented because her supposed degeneration is of the mind rather than of the body, and also because she reappears in the social foreground of the novel after she has perished symbolically in the scene in the wood. James uses restrainedly the same kind of descriptive figures that pertain to Brissenden to characterize Mrs. Server. She, too, is the dead or dying who struggles to keep up appearances. In the portrait gallery the narrator's description of her delicate beauty is tinctured with the idea of death: "She might have been herself . . . an old dead pastel under glass" (51). Just as Brissenden is "fatigued, fixed, settled," Mrs. Server is "arranged and arrayed, disguised and decorated" (96), language with funereal connotations in this context. If Brissenden cannot conceal the stoop of his shoulders or the perpetual signs of aging, Mrs. Server must account for "the snapped cord of her faculty of talk. Guy Brissenden had, at the worst, his compromised face and figure to show and to shroud. . . . She had her whole compromised machinery of thought and speech, and if these signs were not, like his, external, that made her case but the harder, for she had to create, with intelligence rapidly ebbing, with wit half gone, the illusion of an unimpaired estate" (96–7). The sense in which Mrs. Server symbolically perishes will presently be made clearer, but such passages as these from the scene in the wood attest figuratively to the fact:

She was the absolute wreck of her storm, accordingly, but to which the pale ghost of a special sensibility still clung, waving from the mast, with a bravery that went to the heart, the last tatter of its flag. (137)

[Briss and Mrs. Server] each had, by their unprecedented plight, something for the other, some intimacy of unspeakable confidence, that no one else in the world could have for either. They had been feeling their way to it, but at the end of their fitful day they had grown confusedly, yet beneficently sure. The explanation here again was simple—they had the sense of a common fate. (140)

To convey the idea of the dissolution of Mrs. Server's faculties, James relies more heavily on stylized symptoms of decay than with Brissenden, meanwhile reserving descriptive passages for the narrator's celebration of her beauty and charm of manner. Hence her distraction finds expression in the motif of the bee that flits without rest from one to another: " 'With what intensity . . . she has kept alighting' " (61), Obert observes. She seems to be " 'all over the place' " to Mrs. Brissenden (75), as well as to the narrator (82). And the narrator remarks that she appears with different gentlemen "in settings separated by such intervals that [he] wondered at the celerity with which she proceeded from spot to spot (91). The second stylized symptom of what the narrator takes to be May's intellectual dissolution is her forced smile, and to trace its appearances is to come to the heart of the symbolism in *The Sacred Fount*.

In interpreting May's smile the mysterious portrait is again a key. When she and the narrator stand before it, he cannot see the grimace in the mask; to him, though the mask is " 'extremely studied,' " it is " 'charmingly pretty' " (56). But Mrs. Server can see nothing else; to her this is a " 'grinning mask' " (56), a descriptive phrase which may evoke the

idea of a grinning skull. At this moment Mrs. Server appeals
to Ford Obert, who introduces the sequence of remarks that
identifies the mask with Mrs. Server herself. It is in the light
of this identification, I believe, that Mrs. Server's own smile
is to be considered. The narrator cannot see the grimace in
the painting, but neither, in that same chapter, can he see
what Ford Obert insists on, that " 'there's something the
matter with [Mrs. Server].' " " 'I don't myself, you see, perceive it' " (62), the narrator replies. Is the grimace in the
mask that resembles Mrs. Server perhaps then to be taken
as a clue to what is "the matter with her" when a grimace
appears later on her own face? Is some kind of death symbolically recorded in her face just as it is in the mask as she
interprets it? Is her grimace also a sort of mask? And, finally,
what has happened to the narrator when later he can see
May's grimace, though he could not see that in the painted
mask which resembles her?

What has happened is simply what Mrs. Brissenden and
Obert and even the narrator himself have been hinting at
meanwhile; between Chapters IV and VIII the narrator is
falling in love with May, and one effect is that he sees her
differently when he comes upon her in the wood. Here he is
no longer in his supposed role of detached observer but
significantly places himself *in* a picture with her, *in* a tale:
"We were in a beautiful old picture, we were in a beautiful
old tale" (130). It is in these moments that the narrator sees
May's smile as something other than beautiful, as a form
which she struggles to maintain (132–3). Her smile, in other
words, becomes for him a grimace because for the first time
he recognizes her unhappiness, though he may not understand its origin.

As the narrator has observed, passion is the agent of change
within the book. Mrs. Brissenden has presumably grown

more lovely because of her knowledge of Gilbert Long's love. Long has become "the transfigured talker" (106) because of his *affaire de coeur* with Mrs. Brissenden. A similar miracle might occur for Mrs. Server, one supposes, if the narrator would admit his love for her. Within the "old tale" in which he now moves, the narrator has reached the point of decision. His love for May Server is the agent through which she too might be transformed. So long as she feels in this interview that he may be interested in her, she does, as a matter of fact, begin to change. Reassured by his kindness, she relaxes for the first time, and her grimace, the symptom in her expression of her effort to keep up appearances, begins to fade: "She went through the form of expression, but what told me everything was the way the form of expression broke down. Her lovely grimace, the light of the previous hours, was as blurred as a bit of brushwork in water-colour spoiled by the upsetting of the artist's glass" (132–3). She no longer has the sense of isolation, perhaps, which the grimace normally masks or denies.

For the narrator, however, to declare his love would be to deny his theory, for the theory postulates that Mrs. Server is not available to be loved by him. And the theory, the proud creation of his own intellect, is in a sense himself, an equation which he later explicitly makes in the final talk with Mrs. Brissenden (288). Hence, to love May is to deny himself, the part of himself at least of which he is most proud, and this the narrator cannot bring himself to do. He therefore remains silent, and May's metamorphosis is arrested. The "terrible little fixed smile" (148) returns—"the heart-breaking facial contortion . . . by which she imagined herself to represent the pleasant give-and-take of society" (149)—as the moments when the narrator could have spoken slip away.

What Mrs. Server's grimace seems to represent, therefore

(and Mrs. Server herself), is not so much the death of the intellect, as the narrator would have it, as the death of the heart. Mrs. Server has endured some process of disillusion and resignation comparable to that which Isabel Archer experienced in an unhappy marriage and in the loss of her child; and like Isabel, May Server has assumed an artificial attitude for practical purposes: "If [Isabel] wore a mask, it completely covered her face. There was something fixed and mechanical in the serenity painted upon it; this was not an expression, Ralph said—it was a representation. . . . 'What did Isabel represent?' Ralph asked himself; and he could only answer by saying that she represented Gilbert Osmond." [8] Mrs. Server's mask, on the other hand, is presumably the representation of happiness (122), of well-being, since her problem, unlike Isabel's, is to find a new match rather than to endure an old one. The narrator offered a chance which has failed her, and by midnight she regains a certain degree of equilibrium, to which Ford Obert testifies (212–4). Yet the disguise remains intact when she appears on stage the last time: "Mrs. Server's unquenchable little smile had never yet been so far from quenched" (195).

Meanwhile the narrator, having made his choice, goes on to celebrate the eventual perfecting of his theory even at the cost of losing his compassion for May Server and for Brissenden:

And I could only say to myself that this was the price—the price of the secret success, the lonely liberty and the intellectual joy.

---

[8] *The Portrait of a Lady* (Boston: Houghton Mifflin Company, 1881), pp. 343–344. Cf. Guy Brissenden's brief account of Mrs. Server's past: " 'She *isn't* happy. . . . Her circumstances are nothing wonderful. She has none too much money; she has had three children and lost them; and nobody that belongs to her appears ever to have been particularly nice to her' " (119).

There were things that for so private and splendid a revel—that of the exclusive King with his Wagner opera—I could only let go, and the special torment of my case was that the condition of light, of the satisfaction of curiosity and of the attestation of triumph, was in this direct way the sacrifice of feeling. There was no point at which my assurance could, by the scientific method, judge itself complete enough not to regard feeling as an interference and, in consequence, as a possible check. If it had to go I knew well who went with it, but I wasn't there to save *them.* I was there to save my priceless pearl of an inquiry and to harden, to that end, my heart.   (296)

The ultimate irony, therefore, is that when Mrs. Brissenden persists in chipping away at his theory during their final interview the narrator is eventually left with nothing to love. Hence not only Brissenden and May Server are victims in *The Sacred Fount* but also the narrator himself because the object of his love has failed him. Belatedly he had seemed to wish to re-enter the "old tale" in which he felt that he moved in the wood, to think of his opportunity as perhaps still lying ahead: " 'We're like the messengers and heralds in the tale of Cinderella,' " he tells Mrs. Brissenden, " 'and I protest, I assure you, against any sacrifice of our dénoûment. We've still the glass shoe to fit' " (260). But here, perhaps, is the symbolic significance of midnight's having meanwhile struck, the hour when Cinderella changed back into the creature she had been. The adventure is done at least for the present, the narrator cannot re-enter the old tale, and whether he will have another chance lies beyond the limits of the present story.

That the narrator retrospectively knows what happened to him is implied in a subsidiary figurative motif. When he first suspected that he was falling in love with Mrs. Server, he rather obscurely recorded his alternatives as flight and making

love to her: "It was all very well to run away; there would be
no effectual running away but to have my things quickly
packed and catch, if possible, a train for town. On the spot I
had to *be* on it; and it began to dawn before me that there
was something quite other I possibly might do with Mrs.
Server than endeavour ineffectually to forget her. What was
none of one's business [i.e., Mrs. Server's business] might
change its name should importunity take the form of utility"
(93). But to the narrator the train is not merely the vehicle
in which he might flee Newmarch; it is identified in his mind
with the "first mystic throb" of excitement he experienced
"after finding [himself], the day before in our railway-
carriage, shut up to an hour's contemplation and collation,
as it were, of Gilbert Long and Mrs. Brissenden" (127). The
idea of the train is associated, in other words, with the initiation of the theory. With these associations of the train with
flight and with the initiation of the theory in mind, the
reader can translate a significant passage at the end of the
second evening. The narrator appears to be making a general
protest against the forms and artificialities of Newmarch, but
he may in fact be recording his particular experience:

I found the breath of the outer air a sudden corrective to the
grossness of our lustre and the thickness of our medium, our general heavy humanity. I felt its taste sweet, and while I leaned for
refreshment on the sill I thought of many things. One of those
that passed before me was the way that Newmarch and its hospital-
ities were sacrificed, after all, . . . to material frustrations. We were
all so fine and formal, and the ladies in particular at once so little
and so much clothed, so beflounced yet so denuded, that the
summer stars called to us in vain. We had ignored them in our
crystal cage, among our tinkling lamps; no more free really to
alight than if we had been dashing in a locked railway-train across
a lovely land. I remember asking myself if I mightn't still take a

turn under them, and I remember that on appealing to my watch
for its sanction I found midnight to have struck. That then was
the end.   (199–200)

Call the summer stars nature, and going out under them
one's natural impulse. Another of the narrator's impulses
would have been to make love to Mrs. Server. His alternative,
he had considered this morning, was to catch a train back to
town. Though he is still at Newmarch, that in effect is what
he did: fled, ignored nature, subscribed to forms, that for
example of not encroaching on what his theory postulates is
Gilbert Long's territory. He wonders if he may still act on a
natural impulse, go out under the stars, but, characteristically, consults his watch and finds that it is too late. (Even
as the narrator meditates he can see Gilbert Long on the
terrace. Long has gone out despite the hour, presumably for
a meeting with Mrs. Brissenden either before or after her
talk with the narrator.) Midnight has struck and that is the
end. Of what? Of the narrator's opportunity. He has missed
his chance, preferred his theory to the lady, and hence been
no more free really to alight than if he individually had been
dashing in a locked railway-train across a lovely land.

The subsequent appearance of the grimace in the narrator's own face is the mark of his choice, for he lives without
love, and struggling to keep up appearances, as Brissenden
and Mrs. Server do: " 'God grant I don't see *you* again at all!'
was the prayer sharply determined in my heart as I left Mrs.
Server behind me. I left her behind me for ever, but the
prayer has not been answered. I did see her again; I see her
now; I shall see her always; I shall continue to feel at
moments in my own facial muscles the deadly little ache of
her heroic grin" (197; cf. 293, 317). The narrator is doomed
to keep up appearances not only with the other characters in

the novel, however, but also with the reader of his "anecdote." For he has had to record his adventure in such a way
that he would emerge with his dignity and his reputation for
acuity intact rather than reveal himself as a man whom pride
led to make a foolish mistake at a great price. Perhaps, after
all, then, he himself is "The Man with the Mask," a figure in
whom the serious and the comic elements of the book converge. For he himself reminds one of a wide-eyed clown, like
the man in the portrait, and yet is to be taken seriously because symbolically he represents a kind of death, the harden-
ing of the heart (296), signified in the grimace which he
shares with the portrayed mask and with Mrs. Server.

Furthermore, the narrator joins Brissenden and Mrs.
Server not only as a victim but also as an emblematic figure
of death, for it is he whose presence and behavior have
elicited those symptoms in both Brissenden and Mrs. Server
which appear symbolically to represent their decease.[9] This
function for the narrator is suggested in a recurrent piece of
stage business. Mrs. Server, "walking alone . . . in the grey
wood and pausing at sight of [the narrator], showed herself
in her clear dress at the end of a vista" (129). And he had
required her to walk down the long intervening space to
where he waited for her: "If I struck her as waylaying her in
the wood, as waiting for her there at eventide with an idea, I
shouldn't in the least defend myself from the charge. I can

---

[9] See the lengthy quotations on pp. 132–134, above. Cf. James K. Folsom on this point: "James shows us by various means that the narrator
is himself the vampire whom he so carefully pursues. . . . He darts from
person to person throughout the course of the story, sucking nourishment from each." ("Archimago's Well," p. 140.) Or Oscar Cargill: " 'I
think,' Brissenden tells the narrator, 'that she's [Mrs. Server is] rather
afraid of you.' And so she is, and so are the others, for whatever con-
struction he may put on their relations. Animated as he is, he is the
death's head at their banquet." (*Novels of Henry James,* p. 293.)

scarce clearly tell how many fine strange things I thought of during this brief crisis of her hesitation. I wanted in the first place to make it end, and while I moved a few steps toward her I felt almost as noiseless and guarded as if I were trapping a bird or stalking a fawn" (130). "She came slowly and a little wearily down the vista" (131). Then Guy Brissenden had to make a similar journey on the narrator's account: "It was in it all for me that, thus, at midnight, he had traversed on his errand the length of the great dark house. I trod with him [i.e., in imagination], over the velvet and the marble, through the twists and turns, among the glooms and glimmers and echoes, every inch of the way, and I don't know what humiliation, for him, was constituted there, between us, by his long pilgrimage. It was the final expression of his sacrifice" (225). The narrator's own symbolic decease will be anticipated by the same business when he himself receives a tacit summons from Mrs. Brissenden: "At last I saw her through a vista of open doors, and . . . I forthwith went to her—she took no step to meet me" (236). Hence proceeds the interview in which his theory and thus his very identity is sacrificed: " 'It's simply that my theory is dead and that the blight of the rest is involved' " (288).

Because of her part in this symbolic reckoning, Mrs. Brissenden, finally, joins the other three major characters as a figure symbolizing death, though she is the only one of the four who is not its victim as well as its emblem. Her functioning in this role, as the one at whose hand the narrator (as well as her husband) perishes, perhaps accounts for the insistence in descriptive passages on " 'her amazing second bloom' " (64), on how she blooms in her husband's presence (41), on how she has extracted an " 'extra allowance of time and bloom' " (29) from Briss. For she as well as the other principals is represented in the mysterious portrait, in the mask which the narrator finds " 'blooming and beautiful' " (56). She is that kind of death whose presence is not manifest, the sort of person whose persistent demands on another may debilitate and absorb him.

James's implicit comment on love in *The Sacred Fount* is not limited to that inherent in the vampirish equations with which he started, equations suggesting that love depletes, though Mrs. Brissenden represents that possibility. It includes, rather, the idea that the act of living depends on the power to participate, through loving, in life. The symbolic comment made in *The Sacred Fount* is reminiscent of an explicit statement Ralph Touchett makes in *The Portrait of a Lady* as he is dying: " 'Dear Isabel, life is better [than death]; for in life there is love. Death is good—but there is no love.' " [10] Conversely, then, life without love is in a sense deathlike. One may, like Brissenden, be consumed by an unequal passion, or he may, like Mrs. Server or the narrator, be decimated by a love unfulfilled or unacknowledged, whether circumstance or his own character bring about this condition. Of the three victims, however, only the narrator is to be judged—only he is made to appear absurd rather than pathetic—because only he could alter his condition if he would. The symbolic statement of the novel is simply the familiar paradox that though love may destroy the self it is also the means of realizing the self. The symbolic statement adumbrated in *The Sacred Fount* was in a more general application to find affirmative restatement in *The Ambassadors* the following year: " 'Live all you can; it's a mistake not to.' " [11]

[10] *The Portrait of a Lady*, p. 505.
[11] *The Ambassadors* (New York, 1903), p. 149.

CHAPTER 6

The Sacred Fount in the Context of James's Fiction

JAMES excluded *The Sacred Fount* from the New York Edition of his works, and therefore did not have occasion to write a critical preface for it. But he did make one sustained interpretative comment about the book, in a letter to Mrs. Humphry Ward. First he dismisses it as not "worth discussing," describing its subject as "a small fantasticality" and the book itself as "the merest of *jeux d'esprit*." He then adds that he "hatingly finished" it,

trying only to make it—the one thing it *could* be—a *consistent* joke. Alas, for a joke it appears to have been, round about me here, taken rather seriously. It's doubtless very disgraceful, but it's the last I shall ever make! Let me say for it, however, that it has, I assure you, and applied quite rigorously and constructively, I believe, its own little law of composition. Mrs. Server is *not* "made happy" at the end—what in the world has put it into your head? As I give but the phantasmagoric I have, for clearness, to make it *evidential*, and the Ford Obert evidence all bears (indirectly,) upon Brissenden, supplies the motive for Mrs. B's terror and her re-nailing down of the coffin. I had to testify to Mrs. S's sense of a common fate with B. and the only way I could do so was by making O. see her as temporarily pacified. I had to give a meaning to the vision of Gilbert L. out on the terrace in the darkness, and the *appearance* of a sensible detachment on her part was my imposed way of giving it. Mrs. S. is back in the coffin at the end, by the same stroke by which Briss is—Mrs. B's last interview with the narrator being all an ironic *exposure* of her own false plausibility, of course. But it isn't worth explaining, and I mortally loathe it! [1]

Unfortunately, James's "explanation" seems as esoteric as the novel itself, for it is more allusive than explicit. But if I interpret his meaning accurately in the explication that follows, his letter may be taken as corroborative of the interpretation of the novel proposed in this study. For James divulges information about the characters which is harmonious with the individual cases I have postulated for them, and in his adoption of the "coffin" metaphor he indicates his constant

[1] The first three phrases quoted from the letter to Mrs. Ward are taken from Mr. Edel's "Introductory Essay" to the Grove Press reprint of *The Sacred Fount*, p. xxx. What follows is quoted from Mr. Edel's "Introduction" to the Rupert Hart-Davis reprint of *The Sacred Fount*, pp. 9 n. and 14. The unpublished letter to Mrs. Ward, dated March 15, 1901, is in the Clifton Waller Barrett Library at the University of Virginia. I am indebted to Mr. Edel for telling me of the whereabouts of this letter and to Miss Anne Freudenberg, Acting Curator of Manuscripts at the University of Virginia, for providing me with a Xerox copy of the original. It is with reference to this copy that I have arranged James's statements in the sequence in which they appear in the original letter.

Mr. Edel also quotes a second unpublished letter, to the Duchess of Sutherland, but he writes that he is unable to make it available to me. His published remarks, however, suggest that the letter to Mrs. Ward is James's more substantial statement about *The Sacerd Fount.*

For other interpretations of parts of the letter to Mrs. Ward, see Mr. Edel's "Introductory Essay" to the Grove Press edition of *The Sacred Fount*, p. xxxi, and his "Introduction" to the Rupert Hart-Davis edition, p. 14; Dorothea Krook, *The Ordeal of Consciousness*, pp. 176–177; Cynthia Ozick, "The Jamesian Parable," pp. 67–68; and James Reaney, "The Condition of Light," pp. 149–150.

awareness of the more sinister symbolic implications of his material. His letter is especially interesting, too, because in it he adopts a point of view other than that of the narrator. Here he speaks either from his own perspective as author or from that of Mrs. Brissenden or of Mrs. Server. Hence his remarks may help the reader to grasp perspectives which are operative but tacit within the novel.

As I give but the phantasmagoric I have, for clearness, to make it *evidential* . . . .

James is dealing in optical illusions, in what the narrator imagines rather than in what actually exists. (Note James's comparable use of "phantasmagoric" in the passage from *The Aspern Papers* quoted on page 165, below.) But in order to be clear, the purely imaginary must be rendered in a perceptible form, in outward manifestations or appearances.

The Ford Obert evidence all bears (indirectly,) upon Brissenden, supplies the motive for Mrs. B's terror and her re-nailing down of the coffin.

Ford Obert calls attention in Chapter XI to a fact which is important for the reader to note. He indicates that Mrs. Server in her diminished state has been turning to Brissenden for comfort. Indirectly this observation of course indicates his recognition that Brissenden likewise has been turning to Mrs. Server. And he is not the only character who has become aware of this relationship. Lady John observed earlier that Brissenden likes " 'to dally by the way—for *she* [his wife] dallies by the way, and he does everything she does' " (176). Most important, Mrs. Brissenden herself has twice shown nerves when she has discovered Brissenden with Mrs. Server.

During her first interview with the narrator Mrs. Brissenden rather markedly insisted that her husband is content and pointed him out in a confidential exchange with another lady, but she was apparently unprepared for that lady to be May Server:

"But he's wholly content! Look at him now there . . . and judge." We had resumed our walk and turned the corner of the house, a movement that brought us into view of a couple just round the angle of the terrace, a couple who, like ourselves, must have paused in a sociable stroll. The lady, with her back to us, leaned a little on the balustrade and looked at the gardens; the gentleman close to her, with the same support, offered us the face of Guy Brissenden. . . . On seeing us he said a word to his companion, who quickly jerked round. Then his wife exclaimed to me—only with more sharpness—as she had exclaimed at Mme. de Dreuil: "By all that's lovely—May Server!" I took it, on the spot, for a kind of "Eureka!" but without catching my friend's idea.

(44)

This passage apparently marks the birth of a new fear in Mrs. Brissenden. At least her "idea" embraces the wish, among other things, to separate her husband and Mrs. Server at the first opportunity: "Mrs. Brissenden, during the few minutes that followed, managed to possess herself of the subject of her denunciation. She put me off with Guy" (47).

Later the narrator aggravates Mrs. Brissenden's uneasiness about her husband. When, during their second prolonged conversation, she observes that Mrs. Server is restlessly playing up to all the men at the house party, he asks:

"What does she gain, on your theory, by her rushing and pouncing? Had she pounced on Brissenden when we met him with her? Are you so very sure he hadn't pounced on *her?*" . . .

"Is it your idea to make out," Mrs. Brissenden inquired in answer to this, "that she has suddenly had the happy thought of a passion for my husband?"

. . . "She may have a sympathy."   (76)

Subsequently the narrator and Mrs. Briss discover Mrs. Server and Brissenden in yet another tête-à-tête. The narrator is unperturbed, because this juxtaposition simply confirms his theory that the victims turn to each other for sympathy, but Mrs. Brissenden is again discomposed: " 'Dear Guy *again?*'—but she had recovered herself enough to laugh. 'I should have thought he had had more than his turn!' " (85) Mrs. Brissenden proceeds to explain an ostensible motive for her husband's being so much with Mrs. Server, that she uses him to cover up her relationship with someone else (86–7), but Mrs. Brissenden may in fact have grounds for doubt of her husband's motives. She may not know, for example, how much he knows about her and Gilbert Long, or she may fear that Briss will meet her indifference toward him by himself becoming indifferent to her. She would be in a very compromising position socially either if he exposed her or if he deserted her. In the final scene of the book her desperate outburst against Mrs. Server as horrid because she has been making love to Brissenden is apparently an unguarded admission of her real belief. Hence she has grounds enough for "terror."

Figuratively speaking, Mrs. Brissenden has killed her husband by absorbing his whole being. Now the body is seemingly on the point of resuscitation. Or else the narrator, newly instigated by Ford Obert, is on the point of discovering the body, i.e., Brissenden's spiritual death and its attendant causes. In either case, Mrs. Brissenden, to secure her own position, must renail the lid of the coffin; she must keep

Brissenden in his place by continuing to absorb his whole being. She is therefore driven to try to cope with both her husband and the narrator.

Lady John supplies the reader with an idea of Mrs. Brissenden's method, and she also sees a part of what Mrs. Brissenden is herself trying to find out. For when Lady John asserted to the narrator that Brissenden flirted with other women, dallied by the way, she prefaced her remark with an important qualification. Brissenden dallies, she said, because he does everything his wife does, but his flirtation doesn't mean that he will cause his wife any trouble: " 'She has him so in hand that they're neither of them in as much danger as would count for a mouse' " (176). In the present instance, Mrs. Brissenden apparently takes Briss in hand after the musicale, for this is the only moment in which they appear together in a confidential, even an intimate, attitude (198). And here, incidentally, Lady John's phrase is re-echoed in the narrator's description of what he sees in this picture of intimacy:

If one of these ["possibilities" derived from seeing the Brissendens together] might be ... that she was looking her time of life straight *at* him and yet making love to him with it as hard as ever she could, so another was that he had been already so thoroughly got back into hand that she had no need of asking favours, that she was more splendid than ever, and that, the same poor Briss as before his brief adventure, he was only feeling afresh in his soul, as a response to her, the gush of the sacred fount.   (198)

Possibly her line in this instance is to take Brissenden to task for flirting with Mrs. Server as a block for any inquiry he might make into her flirting with Long or the narrator. Or possibly she is simply "being nice" to him. In any case, he is sufficiently "got back into hand" to become her errand boy later this evening when he summons the narrator for her.

Meanwhile, Mrs. Brissenden must also deal with the narrator, for uncertainty about what he knows may be even greater cause for terror in her than what Brissenden knows or would do. In this instance, as we have seen, she exercises logic rather than charm to attain her objective. She summons the narrator and assures him that he is mistaken in what he supposes he has observed. If neither Long nor Mrs. Server has changed, then there is of course no ground for assuming changes in their hypothetical opposites, whoever these may be. There is no need to seek a lady involved with Long. And, by implication, there is no reason to doubt that Brissenden is "all right." In this connection, "re-nailing the coffin" might be interpreted as continuing to suppress the evidence that a psychological murder has been committed.

I had to testify to Mrs. S's sense of a common fate with B. and the only way I could do so was by making O. see her as temporarily pacified.

Meanwhile James had to establish Mrs. Server's sense of a common fate with Briss, because she shares the same fate; she too is figuratively dead or atrophied. As we have seen, when Brissenden is in hand or spiritually dead, he accepts his fate, he creates no disturbance. To be "in hand" is to be "pacified." Likewise, Mrs. Server no longer seems disturbed, in Ford Obert's view. But being "temporarily pacified" may only be ceasing to struggle. Superficially she is quiescent because she has given up.

Mrs. Server is *not* "made happy" at the end—what in the world has put it into your head? . . . I had to give a meaning to the vision of Gilbert L. out on the terrace in the darkness, and the *appearance* of a sensible detachment on her part was my imposed way of giving it.

But Mrs. Server is not happy, James says. She merely *seems* detached. It was necessary that she appear so to account for Gilbert Long's being out on the terrace. Why?—because if Mrs. Server *were* having an affair with Long, as the narrator theorizes, that might account for his being out on the terrace after midnight; he might be out there to meet her. Of course she would feign detachment while the other guests were still up. His presence and Mrs. Server's apparent disinterest would render the narrator's illusion *evidential*. In fact, of course, Long could be out on the terrace for an appointment with Mrs. Brissenden, and Mrs. Server may seem detached because she has despaired of interesting the narrator (page 68, above).

Mrs. S. is back in the coffin at the end, by the same stroke by which Briss is. . . .

In the end, however, Mrs. Brissenden figuratively kills off both her husband and Mrs. Server by stating to the narrator that there is nothing wrong with anybody. Mrs. Server has only been making a crude play for Mrs. Brissenden's husband. The psychological murders of the two victims are perpetrated by the denial that anything has happened to them. Hence they are both back in the coffin by the same stroke.

. . . Mrs. B's last interview with the narrator being all an ironic *exposure* of her own false plausibility, of course.

Mrs. Brissenden's concluding argument is more plausible than the narrator's. But her defeat of him does not justify her unsound moral position. Her reasoning is plausible but her position is false, and therefore the apparent revelation of her plausibility is of course ironic, an inversion of the truth.

James's switch in point of view between the book and the letter indicates how clearly he perceived the central situation in his book—the unfathomed complex of relationships which constitute the problem to be solved—as one which takes on a different aspect depending on whose point of view is invoked. In this respect *The Sacred Fount* seems very clearly to resemble *The Awkward Age.* For in that book the central issue, "Nanda's case," takes on different aspects in the same way. To Mr. Longdon, Nanda seems the victim of her mother. To Vanderbank, Nanda seems constitutionally unable to achieve her mother's grace and wit. To Mitchy, she is an object of love, no more crude than he himself and therefore not objectionable on that count. But in *The Awkward Age* the reader knows that he is being exposed to contrasting points of view because no central intelligence consistently stands between him and the central object. His attention is further directed by James's device of naming each successive Book for a specific character whose influence or self-revelation is especially pertinent at that time. And in the Preface to *The Awkward Age* James invites his reader to note his structural scheme, one which is, I judge, analogous to that of *The Sacred Fount:*

I remember that in sketching my project . . . I drew on a sheet of paper . . . the neat figure of a circle consisting of a number of small rounds disposed at equal distance about a central object. The central object was my situation, my subject in itself, to which the thing would owe its title, and the small rounds represented so many distinct lamps, as I liked to call them, the function of each of which would be to light with all due intensity one of its aspects.

. . . Each of my "lamps" would be the light of a single "social occasion" in the history and intercourse of the characters concerned, and would bring out to the full the latent colour of the scene in question and cause it to illustrate, to the last drop, its bearing on my theme. I revelled in this notion of the Occasion as a thing by itself, really and completely a scenic thing. . . . The beauty of the conception was in this approximation of the respective divisions of my form to the successive Acts of a Play. . . . This objectivity, in turn, when achieving its ideal, came from the imposed absence of that "going behind," to compass explanations and amplifications, to drag out odds and ends from the "mere" storyteller's great property-shop of aids to illusion.[2]

The "occasions" in *The Sacred Fount* are on a smaller scale than most of those in *The Awkward Age:* they usually take the form of a conversation between two characters (of whom the narrator is always one) or that of the narrator contemplating and interpreting a *tableau vivant*. But just as the successive occasions of *The Awkward Age* progressively elucidate various aspects of the central situation, so one can discern a similar progression of occasions in *The Sacred Fount*. Especially notable are the opening scene at the railroad station, the only time when we hear Mrs. Brissenden and Gilbert Long talk together; the scenes in the portrait gallery (IV) and in the smoker (XI), in which Ford Obert's perspective is fully developed; those in the Newmarch gardens (VII and VIII), which are given over to Brissenden and Mrs. Server, respectively; and the highly developed exchanges with Mrs. Brissenden, especially the last (III, V, XII–XIV). If James had chosen to adopt the device he uses in *The Awkward Age,* he might have named each chapter or group of chapters for a specific character who especially shapes or dominates the narrator's thought at that point. In *The Awkward Age* there is more drama and in *The Sacred Fount* more cerebration, spun out through these successive

---

[2] "Preface to 'The Awkward Age,' " *The Art of the Novel,* with an introduction by Richard P. Blackmur (New York, 1948), pp. 109–111.

"Acts," but the basic structure of the two books appears to be that of the progressive turning on of different "lamps."

In the Preface to *The Awkward Age* James applies three dramatic criteria to the novel: " 'You have to be true to your form, you have to be interesting, you have to be clear.' " [3] In both novels he realized the first most completely in his astringent pursuit of the scenic method, with its absence of " 'going behind,' to compass explanations and amplifications," [4] but he did so at the sacrifice of clarity and, consequently, of interest for most readers. It is notable that in the letter to Mrs. Ward, as in the Preface to *The Awkward Age*, James takes cold comfort in insisting upon his achievement in this matter of form. But his despair over the readers of *The Awkward Age* must have been multiplied a thousandfold when *The Sacred Fount* was published, and so well disposed a reader as Mrs. Ward was reduced, like the narrator himself, to begging for clues. [5]

The *Notebooks* throw no further light on how James set about developing his material. They indicate, simply, that he began with the equations of the vampires. But the fact that James depicts both Guy Brissenden and May Server in essentially pictorial terms (discussed above, pages 131–134) supports the inference that he initially conceived of the development of his *donnée* through superficial or outward manifestations. Claire J. Raeth has enlarged on this idea: "The Notebook entries for *The Sacred Fount* establish what James meant when he described it as intended only as a short story. Its subject, the *'tenuity of idea'* which James noted,

---

[3] *Ibid.,* p. 112.   [4] *Ibid.,* p. 111.

[5] For some other very interesting points of comparison between *The Sacred Fount* and those novels closest to it chronologically, see Julian B. Kaye, "*The Awkward Age, The Sacred Fount,* and *The Ambassadors:* Another Figure in the Carpet," *Nineteenth-Century Fiction,* XVII (March 1963), 339–351.

places it in the category of the short pieces in which the
interest is not primarily the penetration into a character but
a record of character in its external manifestations." [6]

Presumably his next move was to introduce the character
of the narrator in order to achieve a point of view and a
vehicle for presenting his material indirectly and concisely.
The functional narrator is a stock character of the short
stories of the nineties. Those in "Collaboration" (1892),
"The Next Time" (1895), "Glasses" (1896), "Europe" (1899),
"The Special Type" (1900), and "The Beldonald Holbein"
(1901) are all anonymous, and all exist on the periphery of
the episodes they record, having no personal stake in the
plot beyond that of a storyteller's interest or sympathy. The
narrators of "The Visits" (1892), "The Friends of the
Friends" (originally named "The Way It Came"; 1896),
"Maud-Evelyn" (1900), and "The Tone of Time" (1900) are
hardly more involved in the action of the stories in which
they appear. Similarly, the narrator of *The Sacred Fount,* as
he appears at the beginning of the book, is anonymous, objective, and personally uninvolved in the central action. In
company with the functional narrators, he uses inconse-
quential terms to indicate the triviality of his material and
his own detachment: "the stuff of . . . an apologue or a
parable," an "anecdote," a "riddle." The story-tellers in
"Europe" (1899), "The Special Type" (1900), and "The
Beldonald Holbein" (1901) all tell "anecdotes," for example,
and the whole tone, attitude, and idiom of the artist narrator
of "Glasses" as he first sets pen to paper is comparable to that
of his later counterpart:

[6] Claire J. Raeth, "Henry James's Rejection of *The Sacred Fount,*"
Journal of English Literary History, XVI (December 1949), 319. The
reader will find the whole of Miss Raeth's article interesting to read in
conjunction with this chapter.

"Glasses"

Yes indeed, I say to myself, pen in hand, I can keep hold of the thread and let it lead me back to the first impression. The little story is all there, I can touch it from point to point; for the thread, as I call it, is a row of coloured beads on a string. None of the beads are missing—at least I think they're not: that's exactly what I shall amuse myself with finding out.[7]

I have spoken of these reminiscences as of a row of coloured beads, and I confess that as I continue to straighten out my chaplet I am rather proud of the comparison. The beads are all there, as I said—they slip along the string in their small, smooth roundness.[8]

The Sacred Fount

If my anecdote, as I have mentioned, had begun, at Paddington, at a particular moment, it gathered substance step by step and without missing a link. The links, in fact, should I count them all, would make too long a chain. They formed, nevertheless, the happiest little chapter of accidents, though a series of which I can scarce give more than the general effect.   (13)

The first speaker's personal detachment, his depreciatory attitude toward the substance of his narrative, his analytic cast of mind, and his pleasure in the systematic enumeration of pertinent details, are all characteristics which anticipate those of the narrator of *The Sacred Fount* as he appears in the early pages of the novel.

Thus far James appears to have been launched in a story which was to be fanciful in concept, circumscribed in development, and literally superficial in the rendering of character. His narrator was to be a mouthpiece, and those persons whom

---

[7] "Glasses," p. 85.   [8] *Ibid.,* p. 149.

he scrutinizes either symbols or façades, as Mrs. Server and Guy Brissenden pretty much remain. "The Private Life" (1892), in which the miraculous is left unexplained, is the kind of story that *The Sacred Fount* might have become had James persisted in rendering his material as a short story. Here the reader is led to believe that Lord Mellifont, who cares only for the external impression he makes, physically exists only when other persons are present, and that the novelist Clare Vawdrey has a ghostly *alter ego* upstairs at work on his novels while his innocuous, gossipy other self moves in society. But neither of these phenomena is accounted for. The interest of this story depends primarily on effect, on the external rendering of the enigmatic characters, and extraordinary appearances are left to speak for themselves or to be understood in a figurative rather than a literal sense. In *The Sacred Fount,* on the other hand, James seems to have been working his way toward a means by which he could account for his fantastical equations in realistic terms: The idea of an affair between Gilbert Long and Mrs. Brissenden takes the first of the "vampire" equations out of the realm of the supernatural, and that of Mrs. Server's falling in love with the narrator in turn accounts for her erratic behavior. Hence this story, whatever other failings it may have, is saved from becoming one of the comparatively superficial ghost stories. James clearly thought of this type of story as intrinsically limited. Of "The Private Life" he writes in the *Notebooks* that "the idea . . . is of course a rank fantasy, but as such may it not be made amusing and pretty?" [9]

Such a development of the material, its grounding in reality, would have faced James with a new problem, however, for now he would have to reconcile the coexistence of the fantastical hypotheses that the narrator puts forward with the

[9] *Notebooks,* p. 110.

objective truth presumably apparent to the reader. And this development, it seems to me, points the way to the adoption of an ironic attitude toward his character. For the narrator cannot seriously pursue the false hypotheses without at last rendering himself potentially ridiculous. If, on the other hand, the narrator were allowed blindly to pursue an *idée fixe* while the reader gradually perceived the truth, then James would have a comedy of the limited observer in which the reader's fun consisted in outguessing the narrator. Viewed in these terms *The Sacred Fount* (1901) then becomes—after *What Maisie Knew* (1897) and *In the Cage* (1898)—the third in a series of variations on the theme of the limited observer. For in each of these books a highly endowed observer arrives at an imperfect image of the thing he contemplates (in each instance society in some aspect) because of a specific limitation in himself or his circumstances. In each book the objects of scrutiny—the activities of the couples whom the narrator studies, those of Lady Bradeen and Everard, and those of all the various couples in *What Maisie Knew*—are secondary. And in each book, whatever serious implications the observer's limitations may have, the effect of his misapprehensions is humorous.[10]

Nonetheless, in Chapter 5 I proposed that in its tacit meaning, *The Sacred Fount,* far from being a *jeu d'esprit* or a consistent joke, is a serious book, even a profound one. There is, in other words, a kind of dichotomy between the two kinds of interpretation, "social" and symbolic, set forth. And here again the analogy with *Maisie* and *In the Cage* is helpful, for this same kind of dichotomy has developed in the views of critics of these two novels. A classic instance of disagreement is the vehement debate in *Scrutiny* between F. R.

---

[10] Cf. pp. 10–11, above.

Leavis and Marius Bewley.[11] Mr. Leavis feels that "the tone and mode of *What Maisie Knew* . . . are those of an extraordinarily high-spirited comedy" written under the influence of Dickens; that James is here concerned with squalor but not with "portentous evil." [12] Mr. Bewley meanwhile argues that *What Maisie Knew* generates an "atmosphere of 'horror' " [13] analogous to that of *The Turn of the Screw;* that it is comedy, granted, but "the comedy still has something of the infernal about it." [14] "The comedy of Maisie seems to me much nearer to *Volpone*." [15] Yet, as these critics demonstrate in their unresolved argument, both views are defensible and even cogent depending on which aspects of the book the critic focuses upon. Marius Bewley dwells upon Maisie's plight, F. R. Leavis upon her point of view.

Such divergent views illustrate the fact, I believe, that during the nineties James wrote several "hybrid" novels. Especially concerned as he was during those years with problems of technique, he seems again and again to have chosen a limited subject, one that presumably would lend itself to a humorous or fanciful treatment, only to find himself increasingly immersed in the development and revelation of character or in the consideration of moral implications. These three comedies of the limited observer therefore tend to merge with partially formed statements about choices or with implicit judgments of society. And the resulting hybrids are both light and serious considered on different levels, or

[11] Five articles by Marius Bewley and F. R. Leavis relating to *What Maisie Knew,* all of which originally appeared in *Scrutiny,* Vol. XVII, are collected in Marius Bewley's *The Complex Fate,* pp. 96–149. My citations of both writers are to *The Complex Fate,* introduction and two interpolations by F. R. Leavis (London, 1952).

[12] Leavis, *Complex Fate,* p. 119.

[13] Bewley, *Complex Fate,* pp. 99–100.   [14] *Ibid.,* p. 140.

[15] *Ibid.,* p. 142.

from varying points of view. The inconsistency in tone in *The Sacred Fount* arises from the fact that the book as James ultimately wrote it was consistently developing in a different direction from that implied by his initial concept. Hence the tremendous importance for the reader, as I observed in Chapter I, not to attempt to approach this (or any of James's later novels) from a single perspective, and not to assume that James himself consistently "saw" his subject in a single aspect.

In the present instance what appears to have happened is that at some point James switched his focus from the equations with which he began to the character who was to define and to examine these equations. Whether this happened because he was trying to achieve verisimilitude or because he became preoccupied with the development of the character *per se* is a moot point. Perhaps the idea of Ludwig II began to exert an imaginative influence, a speculation suggested by the prominent part that the building metaphors play in the novel. James frequently uses architectural figures, of course, both in his critical writing and in his fiction. One recalls the "house of fiction" metaphor in the Preface to *The Portrait of a Lady,* or Maggie Verver's pagoda, or the ivory tower, or Nick Dormer's insistence, as he gazes up at Notre Dame, that a poet may build a cathedral of words and a painter rear a cathedral of images: " 'You can rear a great structure of many things—not only of stones and timbers and painted glass.' " [16] But the building figures of *The Sacred Fount* are exceptional because of the degree to which they are developed and sustained. I have not discovered any other comparable *pattern* of figures in other novels. There is none, certainly, within

[16] Henry James, "Preface to 'The Portrait of a Lady,' " *Art of the Novel,* p. 46; *The Tragic Muse* (Boston, 1892), I, 191. (This text appears to be identical with that of the American first edition except for the date.)

the decade of the nineties. And these images do not begin to appear until midway in the novel, concentrating in the second half. Even aside from the architectural figures, there are a great number of coincidental resemblances between the language of *The Sacred Fount* and the material pertaining to Ludwig II: the attribution of madness, be it fact or fiction; the comparison of Brissenden with sovereignty in an opera box; the figure of the house of cards versus that of the glittering palace; the metaphors in which the narrator expresses his desire to enter into a fairy tale or feels that he is re-entering one of the enchanted castles of his "childish imagination" (128–9); and all the various figures in which he casts himself in the role of a collector or a viewer or as the curator of a museum. Especially interesting is James's great emphasis upon the train of lighted rooms in which the final scene occurs after midnight, for the accounts of Ludwig's nocturnal wanderings in brilliantly lit deserted rooms are one of the most salient images in his history. One can only wonder about the degree to which James himself may have been immersed in contemporary accounts of the king and to what extent these directly affected his imagination, but at least one may observe that such resemblances are broadcast in the texture of the novel. It may be that what was at first a casual adoption of some such metaphor or descriptive detail brought the idea of Ludwig II to mind, so that James began gradually to see his figure as an analogue to Ludwig—both men isolated from others, obsessive and megalomaniac in their attempts at self-justification, ludicrous in their misapprehensions, and yet potentially capable of destructiveness in their relationships with others—and that this was the "rank force of its own" [17] which he felt the material begin to exert upon his imagination.

In any event, the switch of emphasis from the idea of the

[17] James, *Letters,* ed. Lubbock, I, 408.

vampires to the character of the narrator launched him into quite a different story from the simple, anecdotal ghost story that *The Sacred Fount* might have been or from the ironic *"jeu d'esprit"* which it did, in large part, become. The principal action of the novel now becomes the narrator's search. The relationships between other characters in effect remain static; e.g., those of the Brissendens and of Gilbert Long, while the narrator's theory is in a perpetual state of flux and evolution. And the activity of other characters is noted only when they are affected by the narrator or his behavior. For this kind of story, which defines itself primarily as a search centered in the mind of a possessed individual, there are, again, notable precedents in James's fiction.

James was frequently preoccupied with obsessed types, possibly because they lend themselves so well to intense and dramatic situations and are intrinsically interesting. Sometimes their obsessiveness proceeds most explicitly from sexual frustration, as in the slight and dated but intense little story called "The Visits" (1892), or in *The Other House* (1896), where Rose Armiger commits a murder in order to remove an obstacle between her and the man she wishes to marry. Sometimes self-assertion, the establishment of one's own identity or one's own rights, lies at the core of such a character, for example Olive Chancellor in *The Bostonians* (1886) and, especially, Mrs. Gereth in *The Spoils of Poynton* (1897). And at other times these characters have some kind of "intellectual" objective, that is, they desire to know, to find out, to discover, an elusive truth. Of course these kinds of motives constantly intermingle within individual stories. Olive Chancellor's self-assertion may have sexual implications, and the argumentative insistence of the narrator of *The Sacred Fount* may be a form of self-assertion. Nonetheless, *The Sacred Fount,* together with such stories as "The Aspern Papers" (1888), "The Private Life" (1892), and "The Figure in the Carpet (1896), belongs most clearly to this last group of stories, whose heroes are possessed with the objective of discovering some specific unknown.

In each of these stories the narrator's preoccupation with satisfying a curiosity, with discovering a truth or a mystery that persistently eludes him, constitutes the principal action. And all of these narrators, like the one in *The Sacred Fount*, gradually become monomaniacal in the pursuit of their objectives. In "The Private Life," the slightest of the four, the narrator is deterred from putting his theory about Lord Mellifont to the test solely because he is caught in the act of snooping:

> If I were to knock I should spoil everything; yet was I prepared to dispense with this ceremony? I asked myself the question, and it embarrassed me; I turned my little picture round and round, but it didn't give me the answer I wanted. I wanted it to say: "Open the door gently, gently, without a sound, yet very quickly; then you will see what you will see." I had gone so far as to lay my hand upon the knob when I became aware (having my wits so about me), that exactly in the manner I was thinking of—gently, gently, without a sound—another door had moved, on the opposite side of the hall. At the same instant I found myself smiling rather constrainedly upon Lady Mellifont.[18]

In "The Aspern Papers" the narrator sneaks into the elder Miss Bordereau's room after midnight, risking the appearance of outright thievery in order simply to ascertain the hiding place of Jeffrey Aspern's papers. He ultimately reaches the point of accepting the "plain, dingy, elderly" [19] Miss Tita

[18] "The Private Life," *The Private Life, Lord Beaupré, The Visits* (New York, 1893), p. 66.

[19] "The Aspern Papers," *The Aspern Papers, Louisa Pallant, The Modern Warning* (London, 1888), p. 137 (American issue of the English second edition; no prior American book publication).

Bordereau's condition of marriage if he may only extract the papers from her after her aunt's death. And, in his compulsion to discover the key to Hugh Vereker's writings, the desperate critic of "The Figure in the Carpet" admits at the end to living with an "obsession of which I am for ever conscious," [20] just as the narrator of *The Sacred Fount* admits to living always with the image of May Server in his mind's eye.

These other three narrators are all as badly behaved as the one in *The Sacred Fount,* who has frequently been taken to task by critics for his bad manners. All of their stories are drawn according to a similar pattern: each one pursues his "idea" to the point where he sacrifices decorum, honesty, peace of mind, or even perspective on the distinction between the satisfaction of his quest and the act of living. In the words of the critic in "The Figure in the Carpet": "For the few persons . . . abnormal or not, with whom my anecdote is concerned, literature was a game of skill, and skill meant courage, and courage meant honour, and honour meant passion, meant life." [21] This sentiment is very close to that of the narrator of *The Sacred Fount* when he equates his theory with his own identity: " 'My theory is dead, and the blight of the rest is involved.' " All of these men attempt to violate mysteries, and all are frustrated because, for various reasons, they are unworthy. They are all case histories in obsession, and they variously appear as amusing, ugly, or almost insane depending upon the specific instances of indiscretion and their consequent effects.

The obsessions of the narrator in "The Private Life" and "The Figure in the Carpet" create more suspense than damage. The narrators in "The Aspern Papers" and *The Sacred*

[20] "The Figure in the Carpet," *Embarrassments* (New York, 1896), p. 64.

[21] *Ibid.,* p. 46.

Fount come to meddle in matters of life and death, one literally, the other figuratively. In "The Aspern Papers" the hunter's ruthless snooping in the elder Miss Bordereau's rooms precipitates the spasm of rage from which she never recovers. And in *The Sacred Fount* when the narrator mentally yields the victims to the vampires as the price of saving his theory, he believes that he is yielding them to their deaths. Furthermore both men, in their respective relationships with the two women who love them, symbolically at least flirt with Hawthorne's unforgivable sin of violating a human heart. The first allows greed for possession of the papers to translate itself into desire for Miss Tita:

Poor Miss Tita's sense of her failure had produced an extraordinary alteration in her, but I had been too full of my literary concupiscence to think of that. Now I perceived it; I can scarcely tell how it startled me. She stood in the middle of the room with a face of mildness bent upon me, and her look of forgiveness, of absolution made her angelic. It beautified her; she was younger; she was not a ridiculous old woman. This optical trick gave her a sort of phantasmagoric brightness, and while I was still the victim of it I heard a whisper somewhere in the depths of my conscience: 'Why not, after all—why not?' It seemed to me I was ready to pay the price.[22]

Similarly the narrator of *The Sacred Fount* eventually chokes every humane feeling of which he is capable for the sake of preserving his theory: "I was there to save my priceless pearl of an inquiry and to harden, to that end, my heart" (296). Each of these men either manipulates or sacrifices the affections of a woman in love with him as the price of the satisfaction of his desire for complete mastery of his "intellectual"

---

[22] "The Aspern Papers," pp. 135–136.

objective.[23] Theirs is the sin that, in James's work, Osborn Andreas has aptly called "emotional cannibalism," "that tendency in human nature to obtain emotional nourishment from indulgence in acts of aggression on other human beings." [24]

All this brings us back to one of the possible ways of interpreting the vampire concept as it operates within *The Sacred Fount*. For certainly the narrator himself is the arch-vampire, though Mrs. Brissenden does her share of the blood-sucking, because of the two he is the more sinister and unnatural in his behavior. It also brings us, by one speculative route, over some of the same ground that James must have had to travel to move imaginatively from the more limited concept of a short story based on rank fantasy to that of a comedy of the limited observer and ultimately to a submerged but subtle probing into a diseased imagination. There is no indication, however, in James's comments on the story that he himself ever traced this process in any such explicit terms or that he saw the finished story primarily as one sinister in its implications. His acknowledgment to William Dean Howells that *The Sacred Fount* "*grew* by a rank force of its own" suggests that he was proceeding intuitively rather than manipulating his material so consciously as he might have wished. And his subsequent descriptions of the book as a *jeu d'esprit* and a consistent joke support the idea that *The Sacred Fount* remained for James primarily a small matter, to be taken lightly as a joke on the narrator. If *The Sacred Fount* is in part sinister, that is true perhaps because James's whole view of life, especially in the later years, in-

[23] See James K. Folsom, "Archimago's Well," p. 141, and Ralph A. Ranald, "*The Sacred Fount*," p. 245, for other statements of the analogy with Hawthorne.

[24] Andreas, *Henry James and the Expanding Horizon*, p. 22.

cluded unsavory and sinister elements. In all of the late books critics have remarked ugly aspects present in worlds superficially orderly and charming, and *The Sacred Fount* is no exception to this general rule, any more than a book as innocent as *Maisie,* or one as limited in scope as *In the Cage.*

Nonetheless, evil is held in check in this book, as it is in all the others, by certain positive aspects also recurrent in James's attitude, and here again the analogy with *Maisie* is helpful. If there is evil in *The Sacred Fount,* it remains implicit. If there are victims, the reader infers their condition from appearances rather than contemplates their sufferings at close range, just as, in *Maisie,* whatever represents corruption is dealt with off stage for the most part. Secondly, ugliness is held in check by irony: the narrator is made an object of humor in his self-delusion; and his ridiculous pride rather than his potential for destructiveness is the focus of James's portrait. Finally, just as one has James's word for it at the beginning of *Maisie* that the child will escape being tainted, so one has Ford Obert's assurance near the end of *The Sacred Fount* that Mrs. Server escapes being permanently marked by her unsuccessful flirtation, that " 'just now she's all right' " (229). This return to normality is inherent in the idea of *The Sacred Fount* as a comedy of the limited observer, for a comical ending required that the narrator should have made a terrific blunder and should be put in his place. As for Guy Brissenden, the reader's sympathies are always held in check by the impression that he is a bore, with all of his taciturnity and premature collapse into stoop-shouldered listlessness. Hence in total effect the book remains within the sphere of comedy or, to come back to Mr. Leavis' phrase in describing *Maisie, The Sacred Fount,* too, might be characterized as Dickensian comedy, in which pathos is a prominent ingredient but the prevailing tone humorous.

In the experimental period, then, ironic laughter is a check on "horror." But during these years James was working his way toward a much more affirmative attitude than that of the nineties. In several of the latest stories, including the three last major novels, there is a positive affirmation of life, or at least of the will to live life wholly and fully. *The Sacred Fount,* more than any other book of the nineties, marks this transition, for it is a negative statement of a positive theme, an adjuration against the "wasting of life." The editors of the *Notebooks* point out that James was consistently preoccupied with the idea of what might have been: "In a few cases James proceeded in the way habitual to Hawthorne, that is to say he started with an abstraction and sought an embodiment for it. 'What is there,' he asked himself, 'in the idea of *Too late* —of some friendship or passion or bond—some affection long desired and waited for?' " [25] Meditating on this theme for use in "The Friends of the Friends" in February 1895, James wrote what might in a different context be taken as a description of the relationship I have postulated between the narrator and May Server: "I seem to be coinciding simply with the idea of the married person encountering the *real* mate, etc.; but that is not what I mean. Married or not—the marriage is a detail. Or rather, I fancy, there would have been no marriage conceivable for either. Haven't they waited —waited too long—till something else has happened? The only *other* 'something else' than marriage must have been, doubtless, the wasting of life. And the wasting of life is the implication of death. There may be the germ of a situation in this; but it obviously requires digging out." [26]

If an adjuration against the "wasting of life" with its "implication of death" is a buried theme in *The Sacred Fount,* it immediately becomes an explicit one in two stories, "The

[25] *Notebooks,* p. xiv.   [26] *Ibid.,* p. 183.

Beast in the Jungle" and "Broken Wings." "The Beast in the
Jungle" was first published in 1903, but James very thoroughly worked it out in the *Notebooks* on August 27, 1901,
about six months after *The Sacred Fount* was published.
"Broken Wings" he had in mind simultaneously with *The
Sacred Fount* at the formative stage, because one of his allusions to the novel and his notation of the idea for the story
are recorded in the *Notebooks* on successive days, February
15 and 16, 1899.[27] James must have written it just after fin-
ishing his longer manuscript, for it first appeared in December 1900. "The Beast in the Jungle" is an explicit rendering
of virtually the same situation as that involving the narrator
and May Server in *The Sacred Fount:* it portrays a man's
systematic, egotistic absorption of the life of the woman who
loves him while he meanwhile obsessively pursues an *idée
fixe*. Whether it is significant that both these victimized ladies
are named "May" is a matter for speculation. The name of
May Server, at least, must have been selected with a certain
amount of calculation. Mr. Cargill observes its appropriate-
ness for one in her position: "Nothing is demonstrable, perhaps, save the innocence of May Server, whose name betrays
the role the narrator assigns her to complete his 'palace of
thought.' "[28] And John L. Sweeney has cogently argued for
the symbolic implications of all the names in "The Beast in
the Jungle," which would imply decided calculation on
James's part.[29] There is another such echo, between the name
Newmarch, the house where the action occurs in *The Sacred
Fount*, and the name John Marcher, protagonist of the story.
Was James possibly making a conscious or unconscious link
between these two stories? In any event, John Marcher's obsession, like the narrator's, remains intact because of his own

[27] *Ibid.,* pp. 275, 282.   [28] *Novels of Henry James,* p. 293.
[29] "The Demuth Pictures," *Kenyon Review,* V (Autumn 1943), 527.

pride and the tact or reticence of others. By preserving his *idée fixe,* that he is a man reserved for some uncommon fate which will spring upon him, he egotistically dramatizes his own importance. The scene in part IV of "The Beast in the Jungle" and that between May Server and the narrator in the wood, in Chapter VIII of *The Sacred Fount,* are exactly parallel. In both the lady is tempted to take the initiative and to reveal her true position at least by implication. May Server, for the first time approaching the narrator of her own volition, silently collapses and momentarily allows the narrator to perceive her unhappiness. May Bartram by a physical gesture of rising to meet John Marcher, tries to communicate her love to him. But neither of the self-absorbed egotists gets the point. Like the narrator, John Marcher loses the lady, whom he belatedly comes to love, and like the narrator (or so I infer), he is faced at the end with a recognition of his stupidity.

The significant difference between the two stories is that James very explicitly states the moral at the end of "The Beast in the Jungle," pointing out both Marcher's egotism and the nature of his new insight in terms that leave the reader no room for misunderstanding:

Everything fell together, confessed, explained, overwhelmed; leaving him most of all stupefied at the blindness he had cherished. The fate he had been marked for he had met with a vengeance— he had emptied the cup to the lees; he had been the man of his time, *the* man, to whom nothing on earth was to have happened. That was the rare stroke—that was his visitation. So he saw it, as we say, in pale horror, while the pieces fitted and fitted. So *she* [May Bartram] had seen it, while he didn't, and so she served at this hour to drive the truth home. It was the truth, vivid and monstrous, that all the while he had waited the wait was itself his portion. This the companion of his vigil had at a given moment perceived, and she had then offered him the chance to baffle his doom. . . .

The escape would have been to love her; then, *then* he would have lived. *She* had lived—who could say now with what passion? —since she had loved him for himself; whereas he had never thought of her . . . but in the chill of his egotism and the light of her use. Her spoken words came back to him, and the chain stretched and stretched. The beast had lurked indeed, and the beast, at its hour, had sprung; it had sprung in that twilight of the cold April when, pale, ill, wasted, but all beautiful, and perhaps even then recoverable, she had risen from her chair to stand before him and let him imaginably guess. It had sprung as he didn't guess; it had sprung as she hopelessly turned from him. . . . He had justified his fear and achieved his fate.[30]

Here, then, is the explicit rendering of the adjuration against the wasted life. This passage is in effect what has been left unsaid at the end of *The Sacred Fount,* though the functions of May Bartram are divided between May Server and Mrs. Brissenden in the novel.

"Broken Wings" is a more circumscribed story than the other two, but it is another very clear analogue, and it illustrates the affirmative note that I suggested is implicit in *The Sacred Fount.* Here once again we have the same story, but this time it is relieved by a happy ending. In "Broken Wings" Mrs. Harvey and Stuart Straith, a writer and an artist, were once in love, but each believed the other uninterested and never revealed his feelings. Years later, both unsuccessful, they find that they can admit their failures to each other, and also their love. Here again the woman initiates the process of mutual self-revelation, but in "Broken Wings" this process is explicit. Of Mrs. Harvey, James writes: "Before his

[30] "The Beast in the Jungle," *The Better Sort* (New York, 1903), p. 243.

eyes there, while she sat with him, she had pulled off one by one those vain coverings of her state that she confessed she had hitherto done her best—and so always with an eye on himself—deceptively to draw about it." [31] And one is explicitly told, too, that Stuart Straith understands her and consequently proceeds to his own self-revelation: "It was not till Stuart Straith had also raised the heavy mask and laid it beside [Mrs. Harvey's] own on the table, that they began really to feel themselves recover something of that possibility of each other they had so wearily wasted." [32]

In "Broken Wings" we not only have mutual recognition in time for it to be of some use, but we also have two persons' mastery of pride as symbolized in the business of removing a mask, a figure which plays so important a part in *The Sacred Fount.* James quite frequently uses the metaphor of wearing a mask to represent the suppression of the real person, and, conversely, that of removing a mask to symbolize the revelation of one's true self. This usage in "Broken Wings" (1900), together with that in *The Portrait of a Lady* (1881) quoted in Chapter 3 demonstrates his consistency over a period of years, but there are other such instances in "The Private Life" (1892), "The Wheel of Time (1892), "Glasses" (1896), and "The Beast in the Jungle" (1903). The mask figure has the same basic meaning in *The Sacred Fount* as in these other stories, though it may have some more complicated ones as well. It is specifically developed with reference to Mrs. Server and the narrator, but all the principals may be understood as wearing masks, because of their identification with the mysterious portrait. Within the social situation in the novel, these masks signify concealment, the effort to keep up appearances that all four of the principals must practice. But symbolically the masks may also be identified with death in

[31] "Broken Wings," *The Better Sort,* p. 19.   [32] *Ibid.,* p. 20.

various manifestations, as I have tried to demonstrate in Chapter 3. Had May Server and the narrator been able to lay aside their masks (which are fixed in place by mutual pride), one supposes that their story would have become that of Mrs. Harvey and Stuart Straith. Or, symbolically, they would have ceased "the wasting of life" with its "implication of death" by ceasing to deceive each other.

Beyond this point James's restatements of the theme of living life fully are increasingly inclusive and affirmative. They do not always define themselves so specifically in terms of fulfillment between a man and a woman, though that implication is always present. In *The Ambassadors,* the first book written after *The Sacred Fount,* Strether discovers, if not a new life for himself, at least the will and the need to live fully. Mme. de Vionnet is a part of Strether's new understanding, and their discovery of each other's essential superiority re-echoes the "might have been" relationships of other stories. But Strether's triumphant affirmation at the garden party is a general injunction to feel deeply and to live with perceptiveness and style: " 'Live all you can; it's a mistake not to. It doesn't so much matter what you do in particular, so long as you have your life. If you haven't had that, what *have* you had?' " Again, in *The Wings of the Dove,* Milly Theale achieves the will to live even after her reason for living is taken away. And thereby she wins Densher from Kate Croy even in death, because he cannot forget the impression made on him by Milly's spiritual victory. In *The Golden Bowl,* Maggie Verver not only survives but also finds happiness in her marriage, when she brings herself to live according to broader and wiser concepts of human relationships and obligations.

Edmund Wilson once speculated that the ambiguity of *The Turn of the Screw* (1898) may be a consequence of psychological insecurity in the author himself, as James pulled himself out of the disappointment and failure of his years in the theater: "Now, to fail as James had just done is to be made to doubt one's grasp of reality; and the doubts that some readers feel as to the soundness of the governess' story are, I believe, the reflection of James's doubts, communicated unconsciously by James himself. . . . One is led to conclude that, in *The Turn of the Screw,* not merely is the governess self-deceived, but that James is self-deceived about her." [33] I suspect, rather, that the ambiguities of *The Turn of the Screw* have the same origin as those in *The Sacred Fount.* Both stories are complicated by a transferal of James's interest from the *donnée* to the observer rather than by a confusion of outlook. But the resultant ambiguities are appropriate to the ghost story, they enrich its effect, while they obscure a narrative which James was to ground much more firmly in the explicable. In any event, there is no self-deception in the author's attitude toward his character in *The Sacred Fount.* James's estimate is patently negative, as the reader's is meant to be. And the inconsistencies and ambiguities of this novel seem most explicable as a consequence of its being written while James's own mind was in a climactic state of assimilation and ferment just prior to the creative outpouring at the turn of the century. *The Sacred Fount,* more than any other book of the experimental period, appears to reflect this transitional state of mind. It is mixed in tone, tending to fluctuate between high comedy and the sinister. It is excessive in its technical virtuosity, for it carries the scenic method to an experimental extreme. And it might have become any of several stories and have had any of several themes, as I have tried to demonstrate in this survey of analogues. It was con-

[33] Wilson, "Ambiguity of Henry James," pp. 146–147.

stantly outgrowing imposed limits, as James intuitively worked toward a deeper and more expansive rendering of the implications of his material. In spirit he was well into *The Ambassadors* before he put down the manuscript of *The Sacred Fount.*

Bibliography

THE following Bibliography contains all items cited in the present study. The section on *The Sacred Fount* includes additional items and attempts to provide a complete listing of notable statements about this novel, including several early English periodical review articles not previously collected. Specific page references are supplied when necessary to indicate the relevant sections of general articles and of unindexed books.

I. Material Pertaining Specifically to *The Sacred Fount*

Editions

James, Henry. *The Sacred Fount.* New York: Charles Scribner's Sons, 1901.

———. *The Sacred Fount.* London: Methuen & Co., 1901.

———. *The Sacred Fount, The Novels and Stories of Henry James.* London: Macmillan and Co., Limited, 1921–1923, XXIX.

———. *The Sacred Fount,* intro. Leon Edel. New York: Grove Press, 1953.

———. *The Sacred Fount,* intro. Leon Edel. London: Rupert Hart-Davis, 1959.

Secondary material

Adams, Henry. *Letters of Henry Adams (1892–1918),* ed. W. C. Ford. Boston, 1938, II, 333, n. 1.

Allott, Miriam. "Henry James and the Fantasticated Conceit," *The Northern Miscellany,* No. 1 (Autumn 1953), pp. 76–86.

———. "Symbol and Image in the Later Work of Henry James," *Essays in Criticism,* III (July 1953), 321–336.

Anderson, Quentin. *The American Henry James.* New Brunswick, N.J., 1957.

Andreach, Robert J. "Henry James's *The Sacred Fount:* The Existential Predicament," *Nineteenth-Century Fiction,* XVII (December 1962), 197–216.

Andreas, Osborn. *Henry James and the Expanding Horizon.* Seattle, 1948.

Anon. rev. *Literary Review,* V (April 1901), 32.

Beach, Joseph Warren. *The Method of Henry James,* enlarged edition. Philadelphia, 1954.

Beebe, Maurice. *Ivory Towers and Sacred Founts: The Artist as Hero in Fiction from Goethe to Joyce.* New York, 1964.

Blackall, Jean Frantz. *"The Sacred Fount* as a Comedy of the Limited Observer," *PMLA,* LXXVIII (September 1963), 384–393.

Blackmur, R. P. "In the Country of the Blue," *Kenyon Review,* V (Autumn 1943), 595–617, specifically p. 597. Reprinted in *The Question of Henry James,* ed. F. W. Dupee.

——. "The Sacred Fount," *Kenyon Review,* IV (Autumn 1942), 328–352.

Booth, Wayne C. *The Rhetoric of Fiction.* Chicago, 1961.

Bowden, Edwin T. *The Themes of Henry James: A System of Observation through the Visual Arts,* Yale Studies in English, vol. 132. New Haven, 1956.

Brooks, Van Wyck. *The Pilgrimage of Henry James.* New York, 1925, pp. 122 and 132–138 *passim.* Reprinted in part in *The Question of Henry James,* ed. F. W. Dupee.

Brownell, William C. Quoted in *Of Making Many Books* by Roger Burlingame. New York, 1946.

Burlingame, Roger. *Of Making Many Books.* New York, 1946. See also Brownell, William C., and Perry, Bliss.

Burns, Landon C., Jr. "Henry James's Mysterious Fount," *Texas Studies in Literature and Language,* II (Winter 1961), 520–528.

Canby, Henry Seidel. *Turn West, Turn East.* Boston, 1951.

Cargill, Oscar. *"The Sacred Fount,"* *The Novels of Henry James* (New York, 1961).

Cary, Elisabeth Luther. *The Novels of Henry James.* New York, 1905.

Dupee, F. W. *Henry James.* Rev. and enlarged ed., Doubleday Anchor Books. Garden City, N.Y., 1956.

——, ed. *The Question of Henry James.* New York, 1945. This volume contains comments on *The Sacred Fount* in the essays by R. P. Blackmur, Van Wyck Brooks, William Dean Howells, F. O. Matthiessen, Stuart P. Sherman, and Edmund Wilson. See entries under the names of these authors.

Edel, Leon. *Henry James: The Untried Years: 1843–1870.* Philadelphia, 1953.

——. "An Introductory Essay," *The Sacred Fount* by Henry James. New York, 1953, pp. v–xxxii.

——. "Introduction," *The Sacred Fount* by Henry James. London, 1959, pp. 5–15.

——. *The Psychological Novel 1900–1950.* New York, 1955.

—— and Dan H. Laurence. *A Bibliography of Henry James.* London, 1957.

Edgar, Pelham. *Henry James: Man and Author.* New York, 1964. First published in Toronto, 1927.

Finkelstein, Sidney. "The 'Mystery' of Henry James's *The Sacred Fount*," *The Massachusetts Review,* III (Summer 1962), 753–776.

Foley, Richard Nicholas. *"The Sacred Fount,"* Criticism in American Periodicals of the Works of Henry James from 1886 to 1916. Washington, D.C., 1944, pp. 80–82.

Follett, Wilson. "Henry James's Portrait of Henry James," *New York Times Book Review* (August 23, 1936), pp. 2, 16.

——. "The Simplicity of Henry James," *American Review,* I (May–June 1923), 315–325.

Folsom, James K. "Archimago's Well: An Interpretation of *The Sacred Fount*," *Modern Fiction Studies,* VII (Summer 1961), 136–144.

Gale, Robert L. *The Caught Image: Figurative Language in the Fiction of Henry James.* Chapel Hill, N.C., 1964.

——. "*The Marble Faun* and *The Sacred Fount:* A Resemblance," *Studi Americani,* VIII (Rome, 1962), 21–33.

——. *Plots and Characters in the Fiction of Henry James.* Hamden, Connecticut, 1965.

Geismar, Maxwell. *Henry James and the Jacobites.* Boston, 1963.

Hays, H. R. "Henry James, the Satirist," *Hound & Horn,* VII (April–June 1934), 515, 518–519, 520.

"Henry James." Anon. rev., *New York Times Book Review* (February 16, 1901), p. 112.

Hinchliffe, Arnold P. "Henry James's *The Sacred Fount,*" *Texas Studies in Literature and Language,* II (Spring 1960), 88–94.

Hoffmann, Charles G. "The Art of Reflection in James's *The Sacred Fount,*" *Modern Language Notes,* LXIX (November 1954), 507–508. This article is incorporated into Mr. Hoffmann's book, *The Short Novels of Henry James.*

——. *The Short Novels of Henry James.* New York, 1957.

Holland, Laurence Bedwell. *The Expense of Vision.* Princeton, 1964.

Hound & Horn, VII (April–June 1943). This volume contains comments on *The Sacred Fount* in the essays by H. R. Hays and Edmund Wilson. See entries under names of these authors.

Howells, William Dean. "Mr. Henry James's Later Work," *North American Review,* CLXXVI (January 1903), 125–137, specifically pp. 134–136. Reprinted in *The Question of Henry James,* ed. F. W. Dupee.

James, Henry. Letter to William Dean Howells, August 9, 1900, *The Letters of Henry James,* ed. Percy Lubbock. 2 vols. New York, 1920, I, 356–357.

——. Letter to William Dean Howells, December 11, 1902, *The Letters of Henry James,* ed. Percy Lubbock. 2 vols. New York, 1920, I, 408–409.

——. Unpublished letter to the Duchess of Sutherland. See quotations in Leon Edel, "An Introductory Essay," *The Sacred Fount* by Henry James. New York, 1953, p. xxx.

——. Unpublished letter to Mrs. Humphry Ward. See quotations in Leon Edel, "An Introductory Essay," *The Sacred Fount* by Henry James, New York, 1953, and Leon Edel, "Introduction,"

The Sacred Fount by Henry James, London, 1959, pp. 9 n., 14.
See also pp. 144–145 of the present study.

——. *The Notebooks of Henry James,* ed. F. O. Matthiessen and Kenneth B. Murdock. New York, 1947.

Jefferson, D. W. *Henry James.* New York, 1961. First published in Edinburgh, 1960.

——. *Henry James and the Modern Reader.* New York, 1964. Also Edinburgh, 1964.

Kaye, Julian B. *"The Awkward Age, The Sacred Fount,* and *The Ambassadors:* Another Figure in the Carpet," *Nineteenth-Century Fiction,* XVII (March 1963), 339–351.

Krook, Dorothea. " 'The Sacred Fount,' " *The Ordeal of Consciousness in Henry James.* Cambridge, England, 1962.

Laurence, Dan H. See Edel, Leon, and Dan H. Laurence.

L[ittell], P[hilip]. "Books and Things," *New Republic,* III (July 3, 1915), 234. Reprinted under the title "The Middle Years" in *Books and Things* (New York, 1919), p. 224.

L.R.F.O., "The Sacred Fount," *The Speaker,* N.S. III (February 23, 1901), 580–581.

Marks, Robert. *James's Later Novels.* New York, 1960, p. 13.

Matthiessen, F. O. *American Renaissance.* New York, 1941.

——. *Henry James: The Major Phase.* New York, 1944.

"Mr. Henry James." Anon. rev., *Literature, VIII* (February 23, 1901), 144.

"Mr. Henry James' New Novel." Anon. rev., *Current Literature (Current Opinion),* XXX (April 1901), 493.

Mortimer, Raymond. "Henry James: 15 April 1843—28 February 1916," *Horizon,* VII (May 1943), 318.

"A Mysterious Novel." Anon. rev., *The Independent,* LIII (March 14, 1901), 619–620.

"New Novels." Anon. rev., *The Churchman,* LXXXIII (May 4, 1901), 552.

"Novels of the Week." Anon. rev., *The Spectator,* LXXXVI (March 2, 1901), 318–319.

Ozick, Cynthia. "The Jamesian Parable: *The Sacred Fount,*" *Bucknell Review,* XI (May 1963), 55–70.

Peck, Harry Thurston. "A Budget of Books," *The Bookman* (New York), XIII (July 1901), 442.

Perry, Bliss. Quoted in *Of Making Many Books* by Roger Burlingame. New York, 1946, pp. 134–135.

Phillips, Norma. *"The Sacred Fount:* The Narrator and the Vampires," *PMLA,* LXXVI (September 1961), 407–412.

Pound, Ezra. "Henry James," *Literary Essays.* Norfolk, Connecticut, 1954, p. 327.

Pratt, Cornelia Atwood. " 'The Sacred Fount,' " *The Critic,* XXXVIII (April, 1901), 368–370.

Raeth, Claire J. "Henry James's Rejection of *The Sacred Fount,*" *Journal of English Literary History,* XVI (December 1949), 308–324.

Ranald, Ralph A. *"The Sacred Fount:* James's Portrait of the Artist *Manqué,*" *Nineteenth-Century Fiction,* XV (December 1960), 239–248.

Reaney, James. "The Condition of Light: Henry James's *The Sacred Fount,*" *University of Toronto Quarterly,* XXXI (January 1962), 136–151.

"Recent Novels." Anon. rev., London *Times,* May 4, 1901, p. 15.

Roberts, Morris. "Henry James's Final Period," *The Yale Review,* N.S. XXXVII (Autumn 1947), 60–67, specifically 60, 64–65.

Sackville-West, Edward. "Books in General," *The New Statesman and Nation,* XXXIV (October 4, 1947), 273. Reprinted under the title *"The Sacred Fount"* in *Inclinations.* London, 1949, pp. 63–71.

"The Sacred Fount." Anon. rev., *The Academy,* LX (February 23, 1901), 165–166.

"The Sacred Fount." Anon. rev., *The Athenaeum,* No. 3827 (March 2, 1901), p. 272.

"Sacred Fount." Anon. rev., *The Outlook,* LXVII (March 2, 1901), 554.

" 'The Sacred Fount.' " Anon. rev., *The Saturday Review* (London), XCI (May 4, 1901), 574.

Seaman, Owen. "Mr. Henry James," *Borrowed Plumes.* New York, 1902, pp. 153–171. A parody of *The Sacred Fount.*

Sherman, Stuart P., "The Aesthetic Idealism of Henry James," *On Contemporary Literature.* New York, 1917, pp. 245–246. Reprinted in *The Question of Henry James,* ed. F. W. Dupee.

Shipman, Carolyn. "Light Reading," *Book Buyer,* XXII (March 1901), 148.

Stevenson, Elizabeth. *The Crooked Corridor.* New York, 1949.

Stewart, J. I. M. *Eight Modern Writers, Oxford History of English Literature,* vol. XII. Oxford, 1963.

Swan, Michael. *Henry James.* London, 1952.

Tanner, Tony. "Henry James's Subjective Adventurer: 'The Sacred Fount,' " *Essays and Studies,* XVI (London, 1963), 37–55.

Tintner, Adeline R. "The Spoils of Henry James," *PMLA,* LXI (March 1946), 239–251, specifically pp. 247–248.

Tyler, Parker. *"The Sacred Fount:* 'The Actuality Pretentious and Vain' vs. 'The Case Rich and Edifying,' " *Modern Fiction Studies,* IX (Summer 1963), 127–138.

Van Doren, Carl. *The American Novel.* New York, 1921, p. 211.

Ward, Joseph Anthony. *The Imagination of Disaster: Evil in the Fiction of Henry James.* Lincoln, Nebraska, 1961.

———. "The Ineffectual Heroes of James's Middle Period," *Texas Studies in Literature and Language,* II (Autumn 1960), 315–327, specifically 315, 320, 321, 324–327. This article is incorporated into Mr. Ward's book, *The Imagination of Disaster.*

West, Rebecca. *Henry James.* New York, 1916, pp. 107–108.

Wiesenfarth, Joseph. *"The Sacred Fount* and the Perspective of Achievement," *Henry James and the Dramatic Analogy: A Study of the Major Novels of the Middle Period.* New York, 1963.

Wilson, Edmund. "The Ambiguity of Henry James," *A Casebook on Henry James's "The Turn of the Screw,"* ed. Gerald Willen. New York, 1960, pp. 115–153. This essay originally appeared in

the Henry James issue of *Hound & Horn* in 1934. It was twice
revised, for the 1938 (New York and London) and 1948 (New
York; London, 1952) editions, respectively, of *The Triple
Thinkers*. The 1948 version of this essay is reprinted in the
Willen *Casebook,* together with a "Postscript" by Edmund Wil-
son dated 1959. The 1938 version of this essay is reprinted in
The Question of Henry James, ed. F. W. Dupee.

Wright, Walter F. *The Madness of Art.* Lincoln, Nebraska, 1962.

II. Material Pertaining to
Ludwig II of Bavaria and to Wagnerism

Anon. rev. *Literature,* II (February 26, 1898), 229–230.

Anon. rev. *Literature,* II (June 25, 1898), 719–720.

Anon. rev. *Literature,* V (December 23, 1899), 615.

The Athenaeum, II (September 23, 1899), 405, and II (October 14,
1899), 509. Advertisements of Frances Gerard's biography of
Ludwig II.

"Bavaria," London *Times,* June 12, 1886, p. 7.

"Bavaria," London *Times,* June 19, 1886, p. 7.

"Bavaria," London *Times,* July 31, 1886, p. 7.

"The Bavarian House of Wittelsbach," *Harper's Weekly Magazine,* XXX (Saturday, July 17, 1886), 459, 461.

"Books of the Week." Anon. rev., London *Times,* September 30,
1899, p. 12.

Cargill, Oscar. *The Novels of Henry James.* New York, 1961.

Clemens, Samuel L. *A Tramp Abroad.* Hartford and London,
1880, Chapters IX and X, *passim.*

"The Court," *Illustrated London News,* LXXXVIII (Saturday,
June 19, 1886), 645.

"The Death of King Ludwig II. of Bavaria" (illustrations), *The
Graphic,* XXXIII (Saturday, June 26, 1886), front cover, 684,
688.

De Burgh, A. *Elizabeth Empress of Austria: A Memoir.* London
and Philadelphia, 1899.

——. "The Romance of a King" [part I], *The Lady's Realm,* III (March 1898), 555–562; [parts II and III], III (April 1898), 685–693.

"The Dreadful Fire Disaster in Paris," *Illustrated London News,* CX (Saturday, May 15, 1897), 665–667.

E.E. "The King of Bavaria," *Lippincott's Magazine,* XII (October 1873), 410–415.

Edel, Leon. *Henry James: The Conquest of London: 1870–1881.* Philadelphia, 1962, pp. 229, 405.

Evans, E. P. "A Mad Monarch," *The Atlantic Monthly,* LVIII (October 1886), 449–455.

Finck, Henry T. *Wagner and His Works: The Story of His Life.* 2 vols. London, 1893.

Fitzgerald, Geraldine. See Gerard, Frances.

"Foreign," *The Graphic,* XXXIII (Saturday, June 12, 1886), 631.

Geffcken, H. "Contemporary Life and Thought in Germany," *The Contemporary Review,* L (August 1886), 277–280.

Gerard, Frances. *The Romance of Ludwig II. of Bavaria.* London, 1899.

James, Henry. *The Awkward Age.* New York and London, 1899.

——. "Collaboration," *English Illustrated Magazine,* IX (September 1892), 911–921.

——. "Collaboration," *The Wheel of Time.* New York, 1893, pp. 99–144.

——. "Glasses," *Atlantic Monthly,* LXXVII (February 1896), 145–173.

——. "Glasses," *Embarrassments.* New York, 1896, pp. 83–180.

——. "The Impressions of a Cousin," *The Century,* XXVII (November–December 1883), 116–129, 257–275.

——. "The Impressions of a Cousin," *Tales of Three Cities.* Boston, 1884, pp. 3–117.

———. Letter to Alice James, June 6, [1890]. *The Letters of Henry James,* ed. Percy Lubbock. 2 vols. New York, 1920, I, 169.

Jones, Dora M. "The Royal Palaces of Bavaria, and their Builders," *Chambers's Journal* LXXVIII (Sixth Series, IV) (February 23, 1901), 199–201.

"King Louis of Bavaria," *The Spectator*, LIX (June 19, 1886), 806–807.

"King Ludwig," *The Graphic,* XXXIII (Saturday, June 19, 1886), 655.

"The Late Duc d'Aumale," *The Graphic*, LV (Saturday, May 15, 1897), 594.

"The Late Empress of Austria." Anon. rev., *Literature*, IV (January 7, 1899), 6.

"The Late King of Bavaria," *Illustrated London News*, LXXXVIII (Saturday, June 26, 1886), front cover, 678–679.

"The Late King of Bavaria," *Saturday Review* (London), LXI (June 19, 1886), 834–835.

"The Late King of Bavaria," London *Times,* June 16, 1886, p. 5.

"The Late King of Bavaria," London *Times,* June 17, 1886, p. 5.

"The Late King of Bavaria," London *Times,* June 18, 1886, p. 5.

"Louis the Second of Bavaria," *Temple Bar,* LXXVII (August 1886), 511–528.

Lubbock, Percy. Editor's note in *The Letters of Henry James.* New York, 1920, I, 166.

"Ludwig II. of Bavaria." Anon. rev., *The Spectator,* LXXXIII (September 23, 1899), 414–415.

"Ludwig's Fitting End," *The Critic,* N.S. VI (July 3, 1886), 11.

MacKay-Smith, Alexander. "The Romance of a Mad King," *Harper's New Monthly Magazine,* XCVII (European edition, XXXVI) (September 1898), 594–605.

"A Mad King." Anon. rev., *The Academy,* LVII (September 23, 1899), 303–304.

Mead, Leon. "The Mad King," *Munsey's Magazine,* IX (August 1893), 526–530.

Moser, Max. *Richard Wagner in der englischen Literatur des XIX. Jahrhunderts,* Schweizer Anglistische Arbeiten, No. 7. Bern, 1938.

"Notes," *The Meister,* VII (May 22, 1894), 64.

[Owens, Marguerite C.] *The Martyrdom of an Empress*. New York and London, 1899.

"The Palaces of an Artist King," London *Times,* June 7, 1890, p. 17.

"Parisian Sayings and Doings," *Illustrated London News,* LXXXVIII (Saturday, June 19, 1886), 645.

"Proclamation of a Regency in Bavaria," London *Times,* June 11, 1886, p. 5.

"Recent Bavarian Kings," *The Saturday Review* (London), LXI (June 19, 1886), 845–846.

Reclus, E. "Louis II. of Bavaria. Or, Romanticism on the Throne," *The Galaxy,* XIX (April 1875), 528–535, and XIX (May 1875), 598–613.

"The Royal Palace," *The Graphic,* XXXIV (Saturday, September 18, 1886), 307.

Scholes, Percy. *The Mirror of Music.* 2 vols. London, 1947.

"The Spectres of the German and Austrian Courts," *Chambers's Journal,* II (November 4, 1899), 772–774.

"Suicide of the King of Bavaria," London *Times,* June 15, 1886, p. 3.

Twain, Mark. See Clemens, Samuel L.

"Urn in which King Louis of Bavaria's Heart Lies," *The Graphic,* XXXIV (Saturday, September 18, 1886), 310.

Vanderpoole, Lew. "Ludwig of Bavaria: A Personal Reminiscence," *Lippincott's Monthly Magazine,* XXXVIII (November 1886), 535–539.

Villari, Linda. "Linderhof," Supplement to *The Speaker,* XIV, Saturday, October 3, 1896), 366–367.

"Wagnerian Letters." Anon. rev., *Literature,* V (September 2, 1899), 217.

"Wagner's Fairy Prince." Anon. rev., *The Bookman* (London), XVII (October 1899), 27–28.

Wirth, Bettina. "A Kingly Architect. Linderhof and Neu-Schwanstein," *The Magazine of Art,* X (1887), 85–92.

III. General

Andreas, Osborn. *Henry James and the Expanding Horizon.* Seattle, 1948.

Bewley, Marius. *The Complex Fate,* intro. and two interpolations by F. R. Leavis. London, 1952.

Blackall, Jean Frantz. "James's *In the Cage:* An Approach through the Figurative Language," *University of Toronto Quarterly,* XXXI (January 1962), 164–179. See also Frantz, Jean H.

Booth, Wayne C. *The Rhetoric of Fiction.* Chicago, 1961.

Cargill, Oscar. *The Novels of Henry James.* New York, 1961.

Edel, Leon. *Henry James: The Conquest of London: 1870–1881.* Philadelphia, 1962.

——— and Dan H. Laurence. *A Bibliography of Henry James.* London, 1957.

Frantz, Jean H. "Henry James and Saintine," *Notes and Queries,* VII (July 1960), 266–268.

Gale, Robert L. *The Caught Image: Figurative Language in the Fiction of Henry James.* Chapel Hill, North Carolina, 1964.

Holder-Barrell, Alexander. *The Development of Imagery and Its Functional Significance in Henry James's Novels,* The Cooper Monographs on English and American Language and Literature, ed. H. Lüdeke. Bern, 1959.

Howells, William Dean. *Life in Letters of William Dean Howells,* ed. Mildred Howells. 2 vols. New York, 1928.

James, Henry. *The Ambassadors.* New York: Harper & Brothers Publishers, 1903.

———. *The Art of the Novel,* intro. Richard P. Blackmur. New York, 1948.

———. "The Aspern Papers," *The Aspern Papers, Louisa Pallant, The Modern Warning.* London, 1888.

———. "The Beast in the Jungle," *The Better Sort.* New York, 1903.

——. "Broken Wings," *The Better Sort*. New York, 1903.

——. "The Figure in the Carpet," *Embarrassments*. New York, 1896.

——. "Glasses," *Embarrassments*. New York, 1896.

——. *The Letters of Henry James,* ed. Percy Lubbock. 2 vols. New York, 1920.

——. *The Notebooks of Henry James,* ed. F. O. Matthiessen and Kenneth B. Murdock. New York, 1947.

——. "Osborne's Revenge," *The Complete Tales of Henry James,* ed. Leon Edel. Philadelphia, 1962, II, 13–60. This story originally appeared in the *Galaxy* for July 1868.

——, Jr. *The Portrait of a Lady*. Boston, 1881.

——. "The Private Life," *The Private Life, Lord Beaupré, The Visits*. New York, 1893.

——. *The Tragic Muse*. 2 vols. Boston, 1892.

Knights, L. C. "Henry James and the Trapped Spectator," *Explorations*. New York, 1947, pp. 174–189.

Laurence, Dan H. See Edel, Leon, and Dan H. Laurence.

Leavis, F. R. See Bewley, Marius.

Matthiessen, F. O., and Kenneth B. Murdock, eds. *The Notebooks of Henry James*. New York, 1947.

Murdock, Kenneth B. See Matthiessen, F. O., and Kenneth B. Murdock.

Spiller, Robert E. "Henry James," *Eight American Authors,* ed. Floyd Stovall. New York, 1963.

Stafford, William T. "Literary Allusions in James's Prefaces," *American Literature,* XXXV (March 1963), 60–70.

Sweeney, John L. "The Demuth Pictures," *Kenyon Review,* V (Autumn 1943), 522–532.

West, Muriel. "The Death of Miles in *The Turn of the Screw*," *PMLA,* LXXIX (June 1964), 283–288.

Wilson, Edmund. "The Ambiguity of Henry James," *A Casebook on Henry James's "The Turn of the Screw,"* ed. Gerald Willen. New York, 1960.

Index of James's Works

Allusions in James's fiction, 91, 117–118, 118–122
  see also *The Sacred Fount*, allusions in
Ambassadors, The, 9, 12, 18, 19, 23, 23–24, 24, 26, 34–35, 143, 154 n., 173, 175
Art of the Novel, The, 17, 36, 154, 160
"Aspern Papers, The," 146, 162–163, 163–166
Aspern Papers, Louisa Pallant, The Modern Warning, The, 163 n.
Awkward Age, The, 5–6, 7, 8–9, 12, 18–19, 23, 26, 28, 31, 34, 120, 123 n., 152–154
  Preface to, 152–153, 154

"Beast in the Jungle, The," 13, 24, 34, 168–169, 169–171, 172
"Beldonald Holbein, The," 155
Better Sort, The, 171 n., 172 n.
Bostonians, The, 162
"Broken Wings," 168–169, 171–172, 173

"Collaboration," 119–120, 155

Embarrassments, 120 n., 164 n.
"Europe," 155

Figurative language, general
  architecture, 160–161
  coffin, 144, 145–146, 146, 148–149, 150, 151
  mask, 137, 171–173
  see also *The Sacred Fount*, figurative language in, *and*, in General Index, Ludwig II of

Bavaria: as builder and artist: brightly lighted rooms of *and* card houses
"Figure in the Carpet, The," 72, 162–163, 164
"Friends of the Friends, The" (originally called "The Way It Came"), 155, 168

"Glasses," 120, 155, 155–156, 172
Golden Bowl, The, 9, 31, 71, 121, 160, 173

"Impressions of a Cousin, The," 118–119
In the Cage, 10–11, 12, 12–13, 14, 17 n., 32, 34, 78, 158, 159–160, 167
Ivory Tower, The, 121, 160

Letters, 103 n., 120
  letters to William Dean Howells, 16, 17, 35, 110, 125, 161, 166
  letter, unpublished, to the Duchess of Sutherland, 35, 68, 145 n.
  letter, unpublished, to Mrs. Humphry Ward, 10, 22, 35, 68, 144–151, 154, 166

"Maud-Evelyn," 155
"Middle Years, The," 114, 115

"Next Time, The," 155
Notebooks, The, 14, 15, 16, 17, 20, 35, 36, 110, 124–125, 154–155, 157, 168, 169

"Osborne's Revenge," 16 n.

General Index